"Revealed are the dark shadows behind credit card misuse and ignorance. Jon's enlightening and exposing research casts a piercing light on irresponsible credit card transactions via the now ubiquitous 'plastic'. A scary eye-opener. Where is it all headed?

- Don Elvestrom, Former Director of Human Resources, The Pillsbury Company

"Credit Card should be required reading for every high school senior prior to graduation."

- Margaret Lins, Former President, Spring Green Area Chamber of Commerce, Spring Green, Wisconsin

"Jon Langione has pulled back the curtain hiding America's greatest and most menacing financial problem, *Personal Debt*. Far more important than the 'sequester' or the uncontrollable spending of the Washington Elite, is the crushing debt being quietly amassed by unknowing American individuals and families. In many cases a lack of financial intelligence is taking American families over a financial abyss from which there will be no return. Those who read this book may be able to escape before it is too late. This is a must read for anyone interested in personal financial survival and success.

- Harry L. Greene, II, MD, Former Executive Vice President, Massachusetts Medical Society, Publishers of the New England Journal of Medicine

The Jonathan Company LLC

Presents

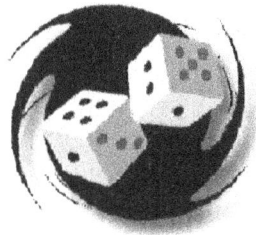

CREDIT CARD

A PERSONAL DEBT CRISIS

Also by Jon and Cathey Langione

Canzio: A Sal Luca Gig

Santa Is Out There, Christmas Tales From
The Edge

Genesis Encryption

Bipolar Passages

Credit Card = A Personal Debt Crisis

By Jon Langione

Art By Cathey Langione

Dedicated To

Harry L. Greene, II, MD

"Friendship is a horizon –
which expands whenever we approach it."
E.R.Hazlip

Chapters

... in for a penny, in for a pound ...*

This is a journey down a road most traveled. When I set-out upon the research I did not know where the path would lead me. The consumer's dilemma as to revolving credit is expressed in the case study of Vado Allacani.

Added to the continuing references of the case study is a family with $16,000 in credit card debt with no way out of the responsibility to pay. They pay over $600 in monthly, late, over-the-limit, and penalty fees, along with the interest. The $600 plus doesn't include the principle payments. They will be referred to as The Family. What appears to be an ease of debt accumulation leads to a psychology of debt and out-of-control spending. My trip to a Debtors Anonymous meeting, my calls to credit counseling companies, and acquiring the statistics that reflect the debt our middle-income population has incurred was an experience into a very dark world. The facts show an extremely high percentage of credit card debtors are in the penalty phase of consuming and charging. I found it disturbing to uncover the lack of understanding of exponential calculations and the inability to compound interest. The average citizen has no knowledge upon which to rely as to the computing of the interest developing into payments of interest; and of interest upon interest. This book explains the mathematics of consumer debt and encompasses fees, compound interest, and penalty computations. It is too simple and too easy to point the finger at the consumer with no assets and overwhelming debt. What I found was a deeper reason that pervades our society, especially the millennials; those ages 18 to 30. The word victim is referenced as to the debtor feeling powerless. Also, the idea of powerlessness, as expressed in the first step of the Debtors Anonymous 12-Steps, is not quite properly understood and is used as a reason to feel the victim. For many of the US population the only inclusion into the capitalist market is consumer credit. It brings to mind the *NINJA* acronym of the mortgage bubble burst of 2008. NINJA means No Income, No Job or Assets. True, there are well-to-do consumers with credit debt, but for the most part the poor and under-employed carry the burden of over-the-limit debt. Those same folks keep the banks in the black with being sentenced to a debtor's prison of plastic. I wrote this for those debtors and more especially for those who have yet to make the choice of signing the application for a credit card with no idea of the ramifications. For they could be signing a contract that states the interest can be raised; 'for any reason'.

*originally with reference to the fact that if one owed a penny, one might as well owe a UK pound as the penalties for non-payment were virtually identical in severity (Wiktionary)

The Dilemma of Vado

"Damn good cup of coffee."

Kyle McLachlan as FBI Agent Dale Cooper, Twin Peaks

It was a dark and stormy night. The rain was pelting the windshield. The wipers could not keep up with the downpour. The BMW splashed through the outside lane on Route 66 coming into Winslow, Arizona. The rain was not running off the road surface to prevent hydro-planning and the car fish-tailed. As he slowed, Vado Allacani knew he had to get off the road but saw nowhere to pull over. Then he saw the faint flicker of a sign in the distance. As he steered toward the sign at a mere crawl another car came upon him and practically rode his bumper. With a splash against the driver's side window the car passed and vanished into the night speeding ahead of Vado at what he estimated was sixty plus.

The sign started to take shape as Vado held a steady course barely seeing the median strip as the road narrowed to two lanes. Vado could make out the neon sign as it grew into focus. 'Ginger's' read the sign posted high above the parking lot as Vado pulled to the front of the diner. His was the only car. There was an eighteen-wheeler far off to the edge of the lot. The diner's lights were bright and he guessed the restaurant was open. At least he hoped so.

Vado made a dash to the front door. It was open and he jumped inside. He noticed a young man behind the counter. To his left was a man sitting in a booth. It was the trucker thought Vado. The young man acknowledged him with a nod as Vado approached the counter.

"Coffee?" asked the waiter wearing a name tag that read Swifty.

"That'd be great," Vado replied. "Are you open all night?"

"Twenty-four seven, three sixty-five," Swifty answered as he poured a cup for Vado.

"Tell you what, I'll have a piece of that pie. What kind is it?"

"Pecan."

"Fine."

Swifty sat the plate in front of Vado. "Rainin' just a tad, huh?"

"Some nut case passed me at sixty," Vado said shaking his head. As he ate the pie Swifty busied himself with cleaning the grill.

Within an hour Vado noticed the rain pattered less on the skylight above the counter. He walked to the front door and looked out. The rain had subsided to a light drizzle. Vado knew he could get back on the road. He stepped back to the counter, "What do I owe ya?"

Swifty went to the register and rang up one fifty for the coffee and two fifty for the pie, with the tax the bill came to four dollars and thirty-seven cents. But, the pie cost Vado thirty-nine dollars and thirty-seven cents, as, with the purchase, he went over-the-limit on his third credit card. The other two were at the maximum. Vado was charged thirty-five dollars on his card as soon as he went over the twelve thousand dollar limit. The interest on the card went from fourteen to thirty percent. Vado's other two cards were topped at fifteen and nine thousand dollars respectively. Vado was now in a situation where he could only make minimum payments on thirty-six thousand dollars owed to Visa, MasterCard, and

Discover. For the last three months Vado has been using his credit cards to make payments on his BMW. He felt he had no choice as the adjustable rate mortgage on his condo went from six hundred eighty dollars to seventeen hundred dollars per month. He wanted to get out from under it but the bank would not accept a short sale.

Vado Allacani's fiscal situation was at a breaking point. His income was steady at forty-six thousand a year. He consoles himself with the mantra of 'well, at least I have a job'. Lately, it has given him little comfort. Vado's personal monetary policy of borrowing and borrowing has taken him to the edge of disaster. In the United States economy Vado is far from being alone. Vado and those like him are what this is all about.

The History of Plastic

"Credit should only be used for something that will outlast the payments."

Anonymous

A piece of pie and a cup of coffee will not outlast the payments when the credit card is over-the-limit due to a four dollar purchase. What is a credit card? In our modern world it is a plastic card representing a bank account that is solely based upon borrowing at interest. The user, the card bearer, is granted a line-of-credit with which to make purchases of goods and services. The plastic card can also be used to withdraw cash from automatic teller machines or for use with vendors that offer cash back as a come-on.

Do not get a credit card and a charge card mixed up. A credit card has a revolving credit line, whereas a charge card is to be paid-off each month. An American Express card is a charge card unless you carry an American Express Optima card. The Optima card works the same as a Visa, Discover, et al. There is also a cash card which is used as currency by the bearer. These cards are now commonly referred to as debit cards. But, it is the credit card that I will zero in on. So, where do these plastic things come from? How did this all get started? (Sullivan and Sheffrin, Economics in Action)

Looking Backward 2000-1887 is a novel of utopia published in Boston in 1887. Written by Edward Bellamy of Chicopee, Massachusetts it is a book referenced by Marxist writers even today. The book posits the nationalization of private property. The book's protagonist, Julian West, awakens into a new world circa 2000. The US has become a utopia. Another character, Doctor Leete explains the society of 2000. As to credit cards, they are mentioned ten times in six chapters. It seems the people have received an allocation of credit. The cards, however, were used as a debit instrument and there is no need to borrow. Bellamy, in the novel, stated that buying and selling were the elements of a failed society. Essentially the book is a precursor of communism that calls out to central planning to cure the ills of a society held together only by the need for commerce. "Materialism is a dark force upon mankind," writes Bellamy.

In the late 1950s I remember my parents and grandparents using charge cards from stores. The cards could only be used in each particular enterprise. The bearer could not use a Montgomery-Ward card in Sears,

Roebuck and Company. The cards looked like a business card with an account number written on them. The purchases were written on a ledger when the goods were checked out at the register. All the accounting was done pencil on paper. It was not a credit device, as in revolving credit, but it was a way to sell goods with a delayed payment due at the end of each month. Bills were not sent out to the customers as they are now to card holders. The bearer had to go into the store to pay the bill, thus, getting the card holder into the store one more time. The accounts were non-credit with no interest applied. I can remember my parents arguing about the amounts on the monthly bills at the stores. Even with a pay-each-month system they tended to over-spend.

Actually the single store cards of the 1950s were a digression from the 1920s and 1930s in which a multiple of stores offered the cards. But those cards had amounts of credit listed on them to be deducted from the amount each month as with a modern debit card. The paper cards were easily copied and counterfeited. Also, with so many bank failures during the Depression the cards went out of favor.

Charga-Plates with embossed identification and account numbers sprang into use in the Roaring Twenties. The transactions were recorded by imprinting the embossed information from the card to carbon paper. *Charga-Plate* was a trademarked entity of The Farrington Manufacturing Company. The plates were used by steady customers in major retail chains. Often the issuing store kept the plate on hand which, again, limited the use of the plate to one store.

As Paul O'Neill wrote in a Life magazine article in 1970, the credit industry was led by the airlines as they got into the charge card business where a pay later system of fly first was established. The use of the cards provided a certain percentage discount much as the traveler's mileage points cards of today. In the 1940s a score of airlines were in league with the system. Also, the airlines started to offer payment plans for installments instead of paying at the end of the month. This is truly the initial development of the modern credit card with the feature to borrow. In 1948 the cards went international but were still used exclusively within the airlines industry. It was not until the 1950s that the cards were extended to multi-users.

> Paul Schneider and Frank McNamara were the founders of Diner's Club. "The concept of customers paying different merchants using the same card was expanded in 1950 to consolidate multiple cards. The Diner's Club, which was created via a merger with Dine and Sign, produced the first general purpose charge card, and required the entire bill to be paid with each statement. That was followed by Carte Blanche and in 1958 by American Express which created a worldwide credit card network." More about American Express later.

It was not until 1958 that the idea and practice of revolving credit came into vogue. BankAmericard came up with the concept. The idea expanded to third-party banks backing the cards. This concept rapidly expanded to include multiple merchants. The cards overlapped the in-store charge cards. BankAmericard was kicked-off in Fresno, California, September 1958. Several small American banks attempted the revolving credit system but they failed. BankAmericard, which later became Visa, had a hard start-up witnessing the idea-man behind the system leaving the company.

According to Jeremy M. Simon in a creditcards.com article, Visa: A short history; writes, Visa was instantly "recognizable in many cultures and languages suggesting universal acceptance. Today, Visa stands for the Visa International Service Association." As of 2006 Visa was "jointly owned by over 20,000 member financial institutions worldwide."

At the same time the card was labeled Visa and the system expanded worldwide developing overseas banking affiliates, in a merger, Citibank went from the *Everything Card* founded in 1967 to MasterCharge in 1969. As per cjr.org writer Ryan Chittum,

> In "1986 CEO Sandy Weill and Jamie Dimon (bought) lender Commercial Credit Corporation, beginning an empire that will later become Citigroup." But, " in 1998, in what was the biggest merger in history, Citicorp (as it was called) combined with Weill's Traveler's Group to create Citigroup ... in 1998-99 Treasury Secretary Robert Rubin pushes for the repeal of Glass-Steagall." In 1999 Rubin leaves for a Citigroup job that will pay him millions of dollars a year. "November 99: Congress repeals Glass-Steagall." And, President Clinton signs the repeal into law.

Further, continuing with O'Neill's article, "Early credit cards in the US, of which BankAmericard was the most prominent, were mass produced and mass mailed unsolicited to bank customers who were thought to be good credit risks. But they (had) been mailed off to unemployables, drunks, narcotics addicts and to compulsive debtors, a process President Johnson's Special Assistant Betty Furness found very like giving sugar to diabetics."

The evolution of the modern credit card came about as a matter of convenience to the bearer; the consumer wanted the card and the banks obliged with astronomical interest rates. So the banks loaded the postal service with offers for cards mass mailed to the general population. This was cited in the UK credit card FAQS in the 2012 online post,

"These mass mailings (of the actual cards) were known as drops in

banking terminology, and were
(eventually) outlawed in the UK in
1970 due to the financial chaos they
caused, but not before 100 million
credit cards had been dropped into the
US population."

Think about it, actual embossed cards related to
the bank account with the receiver's name and an account
number on the card. To activate the card, all the holder
had to do was use it. The FAQS item goes on,

"After 1970, only credit card
applications could be sent unsolicited
in mass mailings."

The mid-Great Depression Glass-Steagall Act
separated banking into commercial and investment
banks. Commercial banks were restricted from investing
the bank's funds. Commercial banks, at the behest of the
person holding the account with the bank, could make a
limited amount of investments but the bank used only the
account holder's money. The investments were restricted
to certificates of deposit-like instruments, and bonds with

high ratings. It was the commercial banks that initially issued credit cards. It was not until 1999 when President Clinton repealed the Glass-Steagall Act that investment banks started to issue credit cards as well. Also, commercial banks began investing their bank's money in a range of products just as investment banks had before the repeal. You would think that the expansion of credit cards into commercial banks, credit unions, mortgage companies, and lender organizations such as auto loan companies would have created competition that would drive down the rates, but as we will investigate this was not to happen. Until those expansions into other financial entities took place, credit cards were limited to the US. It was not until 1966 that the UK BarclayCard was issued as the first credit card outside the US.

Many countries, to this day, are still cash oriented, as with Japan, where credit cards are limited to major merchants as those firms are considered reliable to the banks. Expansion of the credit card systems in the US, UK, and Canada did eventually receive competition from Germany and France as FAQS points out,

"…many cultures were more cash-oriented, or developed alternative forms of cashless payments, such as Carte Bleue or the EuroCard … adoption of credit cards (on the continent) was initially much slower."

It was not until the 1990s that market penetration on the mainland started to expand. This was made possible by the ever expanding technology of computing and the internet. The creation of the seventeen-nation Euro-Zone allowed credit cards to expand by virtue of the common currency. Even still, the development of the credit card had a direct bearing on the reliability of each country's banking system. From FAQS again, as to these bank's reliability,

"France in particular (was) much faster to develop and adopt chip-based credit cards which are now seen as major anti-fraud credit devices. Debit cards and online banking are used more widely than credit cards in some countries."

Credit cards are of a standard size worldwide; 85.6 X 53.98 mm or 3.3/8 X 2.1/8 inches fits a wallet with ease. Handing a credit card to the clerk at the counter was, initially, a product used by high net worth shoppers. Exclusivity is alive today with *affinity cards* used by associations or universities. Of course this is all smoke and mirrors as the associations have a relationship with a bank which hosts the cards. Credit cards are also developed and marketed with special images such as sports logos, rock star's pictures, or even the photo of the card holder. Anything, it seems, will do to entice the consumer.

The old merchant paper cards, the metal cards, embossed plates, and Visa's former BankAmericard are collector's items. Collecting these instruments of credit is referred to as exonumia. And, the cards are traded on collector's sites online.

Announced as a major credit card in 1985 the Discover Card became the credit arm of Sears. Until

2007 the card was associated with Dean Witter and later Morgan Stanley. Discover Financial Services broke off from Sears in 2007, preceding the separation, Discover started to issue debit cards in 2006. Jay Kennedy, the manager of credit for Sears conceived of the Discover card after Sears purchased Dean Witter brokerage and the Coldwell Banker Real Estate conglomerate. Also owned by Sears is the Greenwood Trust Company. If you trace Sears's organization line and block chart you will find that Greenwood is the true issuer of Discover cards. When Discover was created it was attractive to consumers as it had no annual fees attached to the contract. And, Discover tended to offer higher credit limits than Visa and MasterCard.

> "Today, Discover has well over 50 million cards in circulation. And for those who (think) about their cards (as) having limited acceptance, that no longer holds true ... now, over 90% of US merchants who accept Visa/MasterCard also take Discover ... Discover acquired (the) Diners

Club payment network in 2008," as can be read in a 2012 creditcardsforum.com article.

The International Global Operations Headquarters for MasterCard sits in Purchase, New York. The Global Operations Headquarters sits in O'Fallon, Missouri near Saint Louis. This may sound confusing as International Global is rather redundant. However, as to the states the credit card firms headquarter in, there is a rationale and a reason that has a bearing on interest rates and fees. The firm, known as MasterCard Incorporated, is traded on the New York Stock Exchange under the symbol MA. MasterCard was originally known as MasterCharge. The firm began operations in the mid-1960s. MasterCard has a very deep and confusing association with banks from Wells Fargo to United California Bank to Crocker National Bank to New York's Marine Midland Bank now known as HSBC. In 1969 the aforementioned *Everything Card* merged with MasterCard. MasterCard is the biggest competitor of Visa and the evolutions of the two cards went hand and hand. Should you receive MasterCard solicitations in your mail box you will notice that the card will be issued by one of MasterCard's *25,000* worldwide affiliates?

"I don't want to belong to a club that will accept me as a member."

Groucho Marx

The behemoth of the international credit card system is the right of passage for all credit card holders; American Express. Michael Lewis, perhaps the best known author for the retail investor and lay financial talk, in his book *The Money Culture* (Horton 1991), describes American Express as an advertiser with an exotic lilt and he calls AmEx the "financial Kama sutra." He quotes AmEx literature pertaining to the charge card, not the AmEx Optima credit card likened unto Visa and MasterCard, as saying, "Experience the Flexibility of No Pre-set Spending Limits." That is true to a point. Perhaps a SANDALS vacation can be charged, but don't try to purchase a Corvette. Also, the AmEx brochures say, "Verify and Record Expenses with Country Club billing." Essentially AmEx is a snob outfit that tends to its own affairs. AmEx does not franchise as do Visa, and

MasterCard. The AmEx charge cards and AmEx Optima credit card holders are charged an annual fee. AmEx charge cards advertisements promote no interest payments if the monthly bill is paid in-full. But, if you pay Visa, MasterCard, and Discover, in-full, within the billing period, there are no interest payments. Plus, most credit card issuers, but not all, charge no annual fee.

At the outset of the marketing of the AmEx card, high-end stores, through AmEx, advertised that the stores only took AmEx. Stores such as Fifth Avenue and Rodeo Drive retailers were among them. That was because, in the beginning, AmEx was issued only to the up-scale card holder. When AmEx started to send out applications to the middle-income population those exclusive stores brought Visa and MasterCard on board. Also, AmEx promotes "Complimentary … Membership in … Exclusive Private … Clubs." "I defer to Groucho Marx," writes Lewis.

Lewis continues, "Thorstein Veblen explained it all years ago: in affluent societies an economic struggle is substantially a race for reputability on the basis of … invidious comparison … one function of the flashy cards is to reflect glory and cachet the cards beneath them … to attract hoi polloi, like celebrities at a fund raiser."

The article also points to the amount the merchant is charged for the use of the card. Give a shop owner the option of Visa or AmEx and the choice will be Visa. AmEx charges businesses a higher rate for the use of the card. And as time went by the cards became more exclusive and more expensive as the colors went from green to gold to platinum. The annual fees are $55 up.

Ben Woolsey writes in a creditcards.com item, "in an effort to cater to the upper echelon of business travel … its platinum card debuted in the 1990s" … AmEx also has "the exclusive black card, which isn't publically advertized, but issued by invitation only to the wealthy and famous."

However, in defense of AmEx, if a tourist is overseas, and is having financial difficulties getting home, the AmEx office is the place to go. The traveler will receive more help there than the US Embassy. When it comes to world travel the mantra is true, "Don't leave home without it."

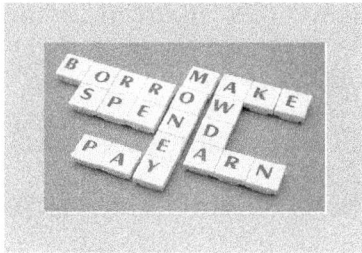

Economics of Borrowing

*"The process by which banks
create money is so simple the mind is repelled."*
John Kenneth Galbraith

The real economic crisis faced by modern nations and more specifically the US is debt. Debt caused by banks too big to fail, debt caused by the Federal Reserve borrowing, and rampant consumer debt with a trillion dollars wrapped up in credit cards. The Federal Reserve sets monetary policy for both the US and the world as the dollar is this planet's reserve currency. The crisis comes about because of the method by which capital is moved within the economy. As Chris Martenson in *The Crash Course* explains, "All money is loaned into existence." Banking has always been about borrowing. All borrowing or the extending of credit to businesses and governments comes via banking. Even if a private investor takes on a block of private company stock the transaction is accomplished by a bank or a hedge fund which is an exclusive name for an investment bank. David Walker, the former US comptroller, stated that, "Too many Americans are following the bad example of their government." And President Reagan was shown to point out in the documentary *I.O.U.S.A.* that Americans are "mortgaging the future for the convenience of the present." I.O.U.S.A. goes on to point out several cogent points.

> The US "does not take action until the problem becomes a crisis." And the crises are brought on by the US

"boosting economic activity", which is a "euphemism for encouraging borrowing." And borrowing is the method used to keep up with emerging nations such as Brazil, Russia, India, and China (BRIC).

The Flaw, a documentary written by David Sington outlines the historical facts that the time frame from World War II until the late 1970s was when the US economy expanded as it had no competition. Then, in the early 1980s BRIC emerged and the result was that middle-incomes became stagnant. Even as productivity increased, wages flattened, and this was to affect the US economy as the gap between production and wages widened; mostly by outsourcing and computers displacing workers. Yet corporate profits mounted. *The Flaw* also pointed out that:

> Executive pay ballooned as did mergers and acquisitions which lead to wild amounts of money in the banks and financial institutions.

Corporations and banks discovered that what they could do with the money was to loan it to their employees. With wages flat the company executives knew that consumer borrowing would expand to allow the middle-income population to keep-up their lifestyles.

From 1970 on the consumer started borrowing against home equity, car titles from quick loan offices, and then the ultimate; the revolving credit card. So, what effect did this have on the economy of the US? It put hundreds of billions and eventually a trillion dollars into retail businesses from car dealers to hair salons. At the outset, around the 1970s, US debt to the Gross Domestic Product (GDP) ratio was at 64%. As of this writing that ratio is now over 90%. From 1995 on, the US citizen thirsted for money to feed their credit card addiction and the public was looking to borrow against the high interest unsecured loans offered month to month. The public was also willing to borrow to invest and did so into the dot.com bubble of 2000. Then along comes the borrowing craze of the mid-2000s that led to the USs worst financial crisis since The Great Depression. Richard Wolff, the author of *Capitalism Hits the Fan* said of the real estate bubble of 2008,

"The greatest economic crisis in 30 years since consumer credit ballooned." He further points out that the crisis is "not really fixable ... all stimulus has failed ... every decade since the late 1880s the working class enjoyed an increase in income ... even through the 1930s until the 1970s." Returning to the wisdom in the documentary *The Flaw* the announcer says, "The credit crisis was caused by smart people doing very stupid things." Also, "while income was falling, house prices were rising, and consumers were borrowing." It was the borrowing against the idea of house prices continuing to go up that created the debacle.

The economics of this, is that, the consumer borrowed and borrowed, and to loan to them, the banks leveraged themselves to heights greater than $40 to $1. Then it all fell apart. "Bank failures are caused by depositors who don't deposit enough money to cover the losses due to mismanagement," said Dan Quayle. The debt crisis cause is reinforced by David Walker as he points out, "too much easy credit for too long can create the false sense of wealth." Then, if the US consumer cuts back on consumption the economy slows and unemployment rises. Yet consumer debt doubles per decade and unemployment may cause the cycle to turn faster as the out of work population uses credit cards to get by.

As of the census, in 2010, consumer debt stood a $2.4 trillion. That totals $7,800 for every man woman and child in the US. 33% of all consumer debt is in revolving credit. The projections indicate that within a few years 173 million credit card holders will have a total of 1.5 billion credit cards in circulation. That is nine cards in each of their wallets. As stated in a money-zine.com item. Even with 7.8% unemployment, or perhaps because of 7.8% unemployment, the amount of credit card debt per card holder continues to rise above $7,000. The banking crisis was a catch-up that was due to happen in 2008. The credit card crisis has yet to hit the bubble-near-bursting stage. Is there a limit to borrowing? It may be when the debt to GDP ratio tops 100%. Plastic cards will then become the at fault reason. The Federal Reserve may well have to foot the card bills of consumers to bring the US out of the next crisis.

The System of Remuneration

"Money is like water,
it flows and recycles."
Canzio Ricci

All money is loaned into existence. When the borrower takes the offer of a credit card the money begins to flow. And, with a credit card, the recycling comes from not paying the full amount when the monthly bill comes due. The phenomena will be addressed as I move along. In the book Canzio: A Sal Luca Gig, Canzio Ricci, a wise guy, brings up some salient points.

"Let's talk about money. What people think about it? How it's used. Who's got it and who ain't? Yeah. That's a good place to start. Lemme see, ya ever hear someone say if I only had more money? Well, when they say that they are reassuring (themselves) that they don't have enough. Even if they got enough they won't be satisfied and won't manage it any better than before and will want more and more. You get my point. Have you ever met anyone that has had enough money in their lives? I have, but ... few. And ya know somethin' those folks were well to do but lived modestly."

What led the US into credit card debt well beyond the means of the consumer? The credit card seeker believes there is not enough money to live on. This sets the future card holder up for the confidence game of being issued a credit card. The moniker confidence game is used to point out that the applicant for the card is confident of handling the revolving credit. Credit cards come into the life of the eventual bearer by two methods. The credit card holder asked for the card or was solicited by a card franchisee. Charles Givens, a Florida brokerage firm CEO and author said that people spend more time choosing swimwear than learning about their own finances.

At one time the actual cards were sent out in mass mailings and the card became active upon the first use. No longer are the actual cards sent out, but about weekly US citizens find credit card solicitations in their mail boxes. That is one way to find an applicant. Open a bank account and the offer of plastic is made then and there. Buy a car and the financing agency will offer the card to the borrower. Go to a store and the offer is there to open a charge account and save 10% on this purchase. Some utility companies offer credit cards. Go to a broker or have an online investment account and a card offer will follow the first transaction. All that needs to be done is to sign the application or in the case of online applications check the box and click the mouse.

The system was not always that easy. In the 1950s and early 1960's the husband had to sign before his wife was issued a card. Often single women were denied credit of any kind much less an unsecured credit card. But the cards have always worked the same. Once the bearer uses it, when the purchase is made, the card holder agrees to pay the card issuer. It used to be when a receipt was signed, but that is no longer true with e-commerce. Statements come monthly in the form of bills or are sent online to the bearer's email. However, monthly may really mean every four weeks which gives the card holder thirteen payments a year versus twelve. So, paying on the first of the month may mean being late by days. This has an effect upon the charges for late fees and interest added to the bill due the next month or in four weeks.

Credit cards are loans with very complicated contracts. For many card holders the issuance of a credit card is a high interest, high penalty, high fee, subprime loan. This means that the bearer of the card can ill-afford to have the revolving credit. Not only does the credit card cost the consumer and the merchant but now the issuer has the card holder believe that the bank is paying out money. This is done by the scheme of offering something back for the card holder. It appears the card holder is getting something for free, but, as with all things, nothing is free, the cost is factored in. The more the consumer puts on the plastic the more rewards, bonuses, and cash back the consumer will get. Along with 0% interest in big, bold print the rewards are advertised in large letters; all on the top of the first page of the mailer. This is where the applicant has to read the very small 6-point type to get the facts. The card seeker will learn that after 0% for six months the rates will skyrocket. Also, the 0% rate is no good for balance transfers as a set rate is initially established for paying one card off with another.

Interest rates set for the card holder have no bearing upon what is charged to the merchants. The benefit to the merchant is that the transactions are paid in full upon the swiping of the card. If a card holder walks away before the receipt is signed or refuses to sign the receipt the charge is already on the books of the merchant and off the books of the purchaser. All the merchant has to do is write 'refused' on the ticket. The benefit to the consumer is that the card is a convenience, and a vast majority, do sign the receipts; not doing so is a rare exception. But the cards convenience can also cost the bearer a lot more when it comes to cash. Cash withdraws are charged a higher interest rate and ATMs are a windfall for the banks.

The following is an outline of the administration of the credit card. The reader will see that there is a myriad of entities involved in the processing of a credit card. This information is derived from dmoz.org.

The Card Holder is the consumer that makes the purchase. *The Card Issuing Bank* is the billing entity. *The Merchant* reaps the benefits of the card yet pays a fee. *The Acquiring Bank* accepts the payment on behalf of the merchant. *The Independent Sales Organizations* resell the services of the *Acquiring Bank*. *The Merchant Account* could be held by either *The Acquiring Bank* or *The Independent Sales Organization*. *Credit Card Association(s)* are the card issuing bank such a Visa, MasterCard, etc. *The Transaction Network* is essentially the server transferring information and could be independent contractors separate from the banks. *Affinity Partner(s)* are institutions such as large corporations, universities, trade organizations, etc, that offer the cards and are paid a fee from the managing bank. And lastly, there are *Insurance Providers* for those benefits of flight insurance, purchase security, et al.

This is all a neat electronic system that can print a mailer, transfer credit card information, or spot identity theft in a millisecond. And those numbers embossed on the card tell it all. The first six digits for Visa and MasterCard determine the bank and the next nine are the account number of the bearer. The final digit is a validity check code, as defined in an e-commerce-journal.com article. Those embossed numbers are a hold-over from an older swipe system that evolved into a magnetic strip. Before the strip the merchant placed the card in a cradle and pushed a roller from side-to-side and the card information was printed upon three flimsy lengths of carbon paper. The merchant would send in the carbon copy and the information had to be placed into the account by hand. The roller system is still used for some merchants that are not attached electronically to the issuing bank. Consumers can see this system at fairs and craft shows. However, systems now exist where the merchant can swipe the consumer's card across a device on a smart-phone and record the transaction the same as in a store. This makes all transactions instantaneous. There is no longer float time for the accounts and the consumer needs to have the credit available in the account or over-the-limit charges will take effect. All the vendor needs to do is set up an account with a commercial card-swipe system.

The Traps of Contracts

"I took the road less traveled by, and that has made all the difference."

Robert Frost

Understanding credit card contracts is not an easy task. It is important to understand how being issued a credit card can affect the debtor's future. This chapter is for the enlightenment of the contract signer and the pitfalls therein. When a potential applicant receives a credit card application, either over the counter or in the mail, a small pamphlet is included. The little booklet is titled Application Disclosures. No matter the bank originating the application the disclosures are about the same.

> "You certify that you are a citizen or permanent resident of the US ... you also authorize us to obtain and use consumer credit information ... we will establish the APRs (Annual Percentage Rates), fees and amount of your credit line."

The pamphlet goes on to explain that the card bearer will have a 25 day grace period within which the card holder will not be charged interest. Note: this is a 25 day period not one month or four weeks. Thus the bearer has to pay the card off within a shorter term than the billing time to avoid interest. Also, interest rates are carried from the first calendar day of the billing period which, again, could be 25 days, 28 days, or one month. And the monthly periods are not always coincidental with the months of the calendar as to starting on the first and closing on the last day of the month.

" … interest charges accrue on every unpaid amount until it is paid in full." This means the card holder may owe interest charges even if the entire "New Balance" is paid but the holder carried a balance over the previous month … *"Your total interest charge is calculated by multiplying your average daily balance by the periodic rate and multiplying the result by the number of days in the billing period … this calculation may vary slightly from the interest charge actually assessed."* (Author's italics)

The interest charge calculations are further expanded upon by stating that the percentage rates at 365 days are rounded to the nearest $1/100^{th}$ of 1%. If this appears confusing it is meant to be. It is easily explained. The card issuer can charge any amount within the rates cited in the contract and, as with the example contract, the rates may vary from 10.99% to 29.99% unless the issuer decides to charge a higher rate. For an applicant with a credit score above, say, 750, the rates may be lower than for someone with a 400 score. That part of the contract is in the small print data about interest. The pamphlet goes on to inform the applicant about rights, expiration dates, rewards, transfer of rewards and general eligibility; which means credit scores.

However, just going to the big print on the application can reveal quite a bit and most of it should scare the applicant away if there is any intent to carry a balance over from one billing period to the other. If the bill is paid-in-full, without skipping a billing period, the contract should hold little fear for the applicant. Pay the bill on-time, every-time, within the days specified in the contract and there will be no interest or so the card holder is led to believe.

What follows is a breakdown of an in-the-mail solicitation, and the contract for, a credit card. The franchisee is a major bank of the 2008 too big to fail fame. The application in the first paragraph states, "Account and Agreement terms are not guaranteed for any period of time."

" … all terms, including fees and the APRs for new transactions, may change in accordance with the agreement and applicable laws. We may change them based on information of your *credit report, market conditions, business strategies, or for any reason.* You should thoroughly review all the materials in this package so that you are fully informed about your credit card loan." (Author's italics)

What this means is the credit card issuer can charge the bearer interest and fees based upon the firm's *business strategies and for any reason*. The breakdown of the interest rates charged are easier to understand on the application than the pamphlet, and, are listed under the applications first section *Interest Rates and Interest Charges*. The rates as defined in the booklet and the interest rates in the contract do not correspond. The big print advertisement on the first page of the contract also does not correspond to the interest rates and the section on the second page. The ad states "0% intro APR on Balance Transfers and Purchases for 15 Months", yet the contract states "0% introductory APR for the first 15 statement closing dates following the opening of your account." Thus, it is not months but billing closing dates. After that, the rate jumps to 10.99%. As to APR for balance transfers the 0% offer is "following the opening of your account for transactions made within 60 days of opening your account." Again, after that, the rate will be 10.99% but the APR will really vary " … based on the Prime Rate." Of course this will be the highest prime rate arrived at during the billing period. Also, the application does not state the percentage over the prime rate to be charged.

The APR for cash advances is to be "19.99% APR for direct deposit and check cash advances and 24.99% APR for bank cash advances." Then in the footnotes it states "any direct deposits completed at the time your application is processed will be balance transfers." The potential applicant then discovers that balance transfers are not 0%. Thus, if the new card holder does not pay the balance transfer in full the charge will be 10.99%. Even if the balance transfer is paid-in-full as soon as the transfer is made, the card holder will still owe a percentage for the transfer. But, that begs the question, why not pay the balance off in-full and make no transfer?

There are penalty fees. Penalties are assessed at 29.99% APR based on the credit worthiness of the bearer. There is a penalty for making a late payment and the penalty APR will be applied indefinitely. Which means the late payment APR will remain and the follow-on charges will be treated with the same APR as a late payment. Following then, is the explanation of penalties in the section for fees. In bold letters is printed *Annual Fees – None*. There are however a list of fees that appear low but the deception is that the charges are for transactions of funds and not for purchases of goods and services.

The application states, "Purchases of wire transfers from a non-financial institution: either $10 or 5% of the amount of each transaction, whichever is greater. *Balance transfers – either $10 or 4% of the amount of each transaction, whichever is greater."* (Author's italics) "Cash advances – direct deposit and check cash advances: either $10 or 4% of the amount of each transaction, whichever is greater. ATM, over-the-counter, same-day online, and cash equivalent cash advance: either $10 or 5% of the amount of each transaction, whichever is greater." Over-draft protection in cash advances is $10 and the card holder is charged 3% for each foreign currency transaction. (Author's italics)

Returning, above, to the italicized *balance transfers* of $10 or 4%, whichever is greater, means that the card holder transferring the funds on a balance transfer will be charged 4%. Thus in believing the 0% ad on the front of the contract the applicant is apt to overlook the information on the second page. Any amount transferred above the $250 mark will be levied a 4% fee. There is no 0% at all for any transaction with the new credit card account. The contract states this clearly with a simple review of the second page.

Under the section *Penalty Fees* is defined a late payment charge of up to $35 and a returned payment fee of up to $25. The contract further states the "Total minimum payment due is applied to the balances with the highest APR before being applied to the balances with lower APRs." Also, on the second page of the application is printed that the minimum APR "will not change for at least the first 12 months of the account. Of course this is based upon the caveats of the *accounts not being guaranteed for any period of time* and can be changed for any reason. The main point of this chapter is the *changed for any reason* stipulation. Signing credit card contracts without reading the information provided, is for many, unfortunately, a road most traveled.

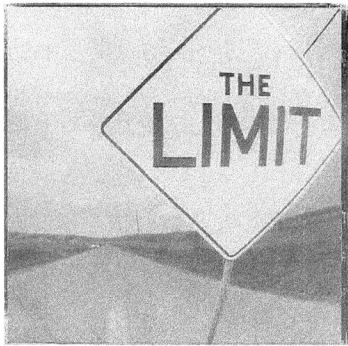

The Limits of Owing

"...money's not the most important thing in life,
but it's reasonably close
to oxygen."
Zig Ziglar

In the case study from the first chapter the over-the-limit credit card used to pay for the pie and coffee will lower Vado's FICO score. When this happens the APR of the other credit cards will go up as well as the over-the-limit card. If Vado is at 30% on the card the APR could go to 40% or higher. Vado is $36,000 in debt to the credit card issuers. If Vado decides to trade-in the BMW, which is not yet paid off, and intends to buy a new car with the payments extended to seven years to get lower than $425 a month payments, the credit cards APR will again go up. Should Vado miss a mortgage payment, again, the APR will go up.

This chapter is intended to be an alert to the consumer to understand there is no limit to owing. There is, however, a limit to being able to pay and Vado has breached that limit. Vado is part of the 56% of consumers that carried over an unpaid balance on a credit card in the last twelve months. Vado is one of those 14.7% of households whose debt exceeds their income. Vado is also part of the 76% who got a credit card in college. Those figures come from the Federal Reserve as reported on statisticsbrain.com.

Hitting the top limits on credit cards is where the issuers want the card holder to be. When the consumer is at the limit, the fees and APRs add up to a great benefit for the banks. A banker once told, now senator Elizabeth Warren, when she was giving a speech to a banking industry conference, that the credit card firms want the weakest customers to be overwhelmed by revolving credit card debt. The remark was,

> "that's where we make all our profits."In a YouTube video about the effect of credit card interest the narrator made a few cogent points. With a $5,000 credit card balance at 18% interest it would take a card holder making minimum payments 26 years to pay-off the debt. The total amount paid would be $12,700 of which $7,700 would be interest.

Remember, all money is loaned into existence and the banks are leveraged, as to commercial loans such as credit cards, to at least a $10 to $1 ratio. So, the bank is not made whole at the $5,000 mark but is made whole at $500. Therefore, the bank makes a $12,700 return on investment for a $500 loan plus $4,500 in principle. $17,200 is garnered by the credit card issuer for a card limit of $5,000 leveraged from $500. I repeat the quote by John Kenneth Galbraith, "The process by which banks create money is so simple the mind is repelled."

Lesley Stahl interviewed the CEO of a notorious predator credit card issuer on a 60 Minutes episode. The CEO stated that the bank, " … used tricks and traps" to get "unqualified card holders" from an "unbanked market" and "more likely to carry a balance" and make "minimum payments of twenty years plus." The bank was singled out because of a huge settlement it made with card holders.

"Compound interest is the most powerful force in the universe."

Albert Einstein

"The greatest shortcoming of the human race is our inability to understand the exponential function."
Albert Bartlett

In the documentary *The Card Game* the writers Bergman and De Granados inform the viewer that interest rates are retro-active on the remaining balance. There are no regulations that cap interest rates. Regulations only require that the fees and rates be disclosed in the contract. The documentary *Freakonomics* points out that high interest is not a crime. The US has no usury laws, only laws against unlicensed lenders known on the street as 'shylocks'. Also, of note, is that business credit cards are excluded from consumer credit card regulations.

The dire situation of the case study, Mr. Allacani, can be summed up in a few enlightening calculations derived from the online site moneychimp.com. The formulas and the results show an alarming amount of debt. As for Vado, it was very easy to accumulate mountains of debt. Easy is the optimum word, but this paper will delve more into the subject of accumulating debt as we go along. In breaking down Vado's finances the reader can see that Mr. Allacani is beyond the point of no return. The income does not match the debt per month.

Income per year - $46,000

Income after taxes @ 18% - $37,720

Income after taxes per month - $3,143

Mortgage per month - $1,700

Car payment per month - $425

Credit card minimum payments per month for a $36,000 balance - $896

Total disposable income for necessities, utilities, etc - $122

Vado has no money with which to live. The only way Vado can survive month to month would be to have the limits on the credit cards raised and use the revolving debt. This, of course, is a very counter-productive idea. The calculations to relieve the debt burden are as follows:

Current debt - $36,000

APR – 30%

Monthly payments $945 (only $49 above minimum)

Months to pay-off debt – 108 (9 years)

Total interest paid - $65,313

Thus, for a $36,000 debt the total amount of funds required to pay the cards in-full will come to $101,313. The case study shows what the limit of owing is, but with an increase in the card's limits, the debt will go higher. Essentially, there is no limit. Eventually Vado would have to sell the house or be foreclosed upon to afford the credit cards. There is a public service announcement shown on the documentary *The Card Game.* A man is standing in his front yard, shows the viewer his house, his cars, his boat, et al, and then exclaims; "I'm in debt up to my eyeballs!"

The Psychology of Riches

"Sometimes when people get what they want they realize

how limited their goals are."

Christina Hendricks as Joan Harris, Mad Men

Malcolm Clark's documentary *Mind Over Money* shows a strange and baffling auction. What is being auctioned off is a $20 bill. The auction has a twist to the rules. The highest bidder wins the $20 bill but the second highest bidder has to pay the amount of the runner-up bid. There are about fifteen students participating in the auction; all do not make a bid. Each new bid crept higher and higher at the rate of $1 at a time. It was as if the students wanted to stretch the bidding out over as much time as possible. The bidding went from seven or eight students when the offer is made for $19 to only three. Realistically the bidding should have stopped at $19, but the three students kept bidding higher. When the bid hit $23 one of the students dropped out leaving only two to continue. The bidding ended at $28 which meant the student bidding $27 paid for nothing and the highest bidder got the $20 bill. The film's narrator asks a few questions for the viewers to think about.

> "Why did the bidding go above $20? What made the third from last student drop out at $3 over the value of the $20 bill? Why did the runner-up stop

bidding at $27 when to continue meant that the runner-up may eventually make the winning bid? How high was the winning bidder prepared to go?"

The students were not asked these questions. The viewers are asked to draw their own conclusions. If two students were of a mind to keep bidding up and hoping the other would drop-out, to what amount could the bidding have continued? Perhaps the bidding could have reached hundreds of dollars. Then the question comes to mind, why take the chance of auctioning to the highest bidder when the bidding could end at less than $20? But, to illustrate the need to win, no matter the price, the psychologist held the auction knowing the bidding would go over $20. The auctioneer garnered $27 for the $20 bill and profited by 35%. 35% is about the amount of interest a credit card holder will accept without reservations. The thesis case study has a 29.99% APR. That is the figure where Vado Allacani quit spending and had raised the debt to the limit. Was 35% a psychological limit for the runner-up bidder? How far would the winning bidder have gone? The idea of the 35% limit is mine alone. Nothing was expressed about the 35% in the film.

The late actor Adam Roarke, when teaching classes at his Film Actor's Lab in Dallas, Texas, often started off a scene preparation by asking the students, "What is your attitude?" And, he also asked, "What is your motivation?" In the documentary *Freakonomics,* the question is asked, "What is the incentive for a credit card?" Perhaps the questions about attitude, motivation, and incentives are answered in a quip by a housewife being interviewed in the documentary, *In Debt We Trust.* She says, "I come from an upper middle-income family and I'm used to a certain level of income."

> She had lost her job. Her husband was the sole provider. They were late in their payments of $16,000 of credit card debt. They were paying $240 per month in late fees and penalties. The $240 was on top of the interest and principle. Computing the interest alone at a $29.99% APR, brought the

total payment, without a dollar of it going toward the principle, to $399, and with the $240 the monthly payment equaled $639. What was the motivation to continue into more and more debt? The answer was for them to maintain a lifestyle. What was the attitude? The wife felt they had to maintain a certain lifestyle no matter the consequences. What was the incentive? Essentially they did so to accumulate more and more material goods or *stuff*. Those three answers led to the idea, on my part, that the husband and wife felt they are entitled to the credit. Henceforth, they will be referred to as The Family.

On a survey taken at the check-out aisle of a local super-market I, for over a year, noticed that on the cover of each weekly issue of gossip magazines a member of the Kardashian family was pictured and written about. Joking about this gossip to the check-out person and the bagger usually netted some dissertation about the Kardashians. It was as if these young people were living a vicarious life through the three ultra-wealthy sisters. Our young people follow the exploits of the rich and famous and ultimately want to participate in their lifestyles. The reality shows of famous people are really following the lives of characters that are famous for being famous. There is little talent attached to shopping sprees and arrogant behavior. Thus, the youngsters at the supermarket, mostly students working part-time, use revolving credit to live like the Kardashians. Or, perhaps think of being in league with the Rodeo Drive jet set.

As mentioned before, a high amount of credit card holders were issued a card or cards in college. Going to college is a time when teenagers are being introduced to a world in which the student is unprepared. Albert Bartlett stated it correctly when he said that society does not understand compounding. Calculating compound interest is not taught to most high school seniors and college freshmen. And, it is these teenagers that the credit card companies target. When the college student applies for a credit card on registration day the card issuer gives them a free t-shirt. (The Card Game)

"The two best marketing tools are free and all you can eat."
Bill Strunk, Banking Consultant

The parents of these college kids often fall into the trap of co-signing the card applications. Or, the student is issued a card without claiming any means to pay for the charges. Often the student is told the myth that having credit cards builds a credit rating for the future. This is somewhat true. When the student builds a high amount of debt or goes over-the-limit on the cards their credit scores sink.

"Human beings respond to incentives no matter how irrational. 0% APR* - they will respond to the 0% and ignore the *." (*Freakonomics*) "Students see credit as a social entitlement." (*In Debt We Trust*) And, to be issued credit cards "students lie about their income even if they have no income at all" The indifference to any requirements for credit, seemingly, by the banks, gives the banks the power to start the student on the road to a lifetime of debt. (*In Debt We Trust*) The concept is for the banks to loan money to the consumer who runs out of money (or in the case of the students who have no money) as a way to build revenue in the future. Eventually the student or the student's parents will begin making payments. (*The Card Game*) By then the cards are in the late payment or over-the-limit status. "The desire for a quick reward trumps rational thought." (*Mind Over Money*) "The students live *for* the moment instead of living in the moment." (*Freakonomics*)

In the mind of the student, is cheating to get a credit card, cheating? This then begs the question, why cheat? Why not be realistic about ones income or lack thereof. Is this the beginning of unethical conduct in matters financial for the teenager? And, will this behavior carry into their adult life? Not only is reporting nonexistent income to get a credit card unethical it is irrational. Irrational thinking is a psychological matter. "The credit card user can stay irrational longer than remain solvent." (*Mind Over Money*) It is a reaction to the need to remain in, or aspire to, the middle income lifestyle. Is this a hormonal aberration? Is being crushed by consumer debt from age eighteen into adulthood a sign of arrested development? Or, is it a sign of addiction?

An alcoholic is a person addicted to alcohol? A narcotics addict is a person addicted to drugs? A credit card addict is someone who is addicted to convenience? Suze Orman, in her book, *The 9 Steps to Financial Freedom* wrote in the chapter titled Being Honest with Yourself.

> "Reality Check: Throw away a three
> dollar magazine you never got around

to reading – easy. Toss in the garbage five dollars worth of food that's gone bad; you may reprimand yourself, but you probably do it all the time. Buy a sweater on sale for twenty dollars, then notice six months later that you wore it only once; it just didn't fit right; you give it away. Now try to rip up and throw away a dollar bill. I have found almost no one who can do this without great discomfort. Yet everything about the way the money establishment functions is calculated to distance us from our money, to anesthetize us to its power. The plastic card that slides through the machine so smoothly when we make our purchases; … (this) 'convenience' leaves us many steps from the actual thing … it's only plastic."

Thus, the mind of the consumer is keyed to not consider the credit card as money. The consumer throughout the month is not spending money. Only two days a month is the actual money value of the credit card thought about and those are the day the bill arrives and the day the bill is paid. And, it is the nature of the consumer, when spending real money, to pay as little as possible. Thus, the habit is developed to pay only the minimum, even if a more substantial payment can be made. The addiction is the convenience of the plastic card and the habit of minimum payments. Making minimum payments will cause the card holder to reach the limit rapidly. Some of the warning signs of credit card addiction are pointed out by Gina Roberts-Gray in her 2009 article Credit Card Addiction: How to spot the warning signs.

"You never have cash in your wallet. You buy things (you don't need) because they are on sale. You have more than two 'branded' or store credit cards. Credit card balances are growing and not being paid down. Your cards are maxed-out (and) you open new ones (for) additional credit.

You don't know how much you owe." In a J. D. Roth Article of 2008 on the *GetRichSlowly* Website, J. D. writes, "Problems will arise when the consumer often does not consider what they are charging on the card." This leads back to the problem of the thesis case study when Vado goes over-the-limit for a cup of coffee and a piece of pie. Also the consumer can "feel like I'm spending somebody else's money."

"When you pay cash, you can feel the
money leaving you."
Dave Ramsey, Financial Guru

For the credit card addict, just as with the cocaine addict, facing the reality of what the user has done and what the user needs to do in the future can be traumatic. Failure to not take action is denial. However, taking action for the cocaine addict is to go into recovery and in two years of sobriety the addict can say "I've been clean for two years." For the credit card addict, such as the thesis case study, after two years of making payments of over $900 a month Vado is facing yet another seven years of debt until he can call himself clean of the debt. Month by month Vado is reminded of the affects of his addiction. For 108 months Vado will recall the compulsive behavior to spend. As Jason Hull, in an article about drugs and credit addiction writes that the addiction is a conditioned stimulus. It is Pavlovian for the addict. And unlike the drug addict who can escape the user environment, the credit card user cannot.

As to Vado the credit card using environment surrounds him. He stands in line at the supermarket and the people in front of him use credit cards. Weekly he sees credit card solicitations arriving in the mail. There are 12-Step credit card addiction meetings he can go to. But no halfway house exists for revolving credit users. He can't even get away from it for a cup of coffee; as some café franchises offer credit card applications at the counter with the coffee house logo on the card. MarksJarvis, in an Arizona Daily Star item writes that researchers have found that as credit card debt is increased by 10%, depression increases by 14%. Applying math to levels of depression is somewhat suspect, but the point is made. Chances are Vado will become depressed as the debt accumulates and well into the pay-off period of nine years. There is a second point MarksJarvis makes and that is that "depressed people tend to spend more."

In recovery the drug addict can get counseling whether insured or not. There is also counseling for the credit card addict. But, the consumer needs to be aware that all counselors do not lead to mental health. In fact Vado may end up more in debt. Is it advisable for the credit card addict to borrow money at interest to pay off credit cards?

The Counselors of Collections

"The model of ownership, in a society organized around mass consumption, is addiction. It is the logic of consumerism that undermines the values of loyalty and permanence and promotes a different set of values that is destructive to family life."

Christopher Lasch

"As many as 75% of clients who enroll in a debt management program do not complete the program." (bills.com) The bills.com Website continues, " ... credit card issuers underwrite part of the cost in a system of payments to credit counseling companies called fair share. The typical fair share percentage was 15%, meaning that "credit card counselors received 15% of all money they paid to creditors on behalf of their customers."

This means that the case study, Vado, will pay an additional $5,400 on top of the $36,000 in principle and the $65,000 in interest. Lender's perceptions of a card holder enlisting credit counseling is the same as bankruptcy; more specifically, chapter 13. Chapter 13 is wherein the income earner, not a business, can keep property and pay off debt over time; usually less than ten years. A debtor will pay fees of about 3% of the loan, after the up-front monies are paid, as the loan pay-off moves along month by month. This means Vado's payments will be approximately $3,480 per month. This is the reason for a high drop-out rate in credit management programs.

Consumer Credit Counseling Services (CCCS) are essentially collection agencies. The idea is that if a consumer goes to a CCCS the debtor is in dire straits and the CCCS is a last resort against complete financial collapse. The CCCSs take advantage of the card holder and promise easy resolutions. A few CCCS counselors were interviewed and here is what I discovered.

A CCCS, supposedly in the northeast, when told of Vado's debt told me that the $36,000 principle owed could be reduced by 33%. Over the phone the counselor stated that the amount could be paid in four years at $511 per month. This is $24,120 paid-in-full for a $36,000 debt. The counselor stated the firm would negotiate away the interest and that the payment would go though the collections department. The counselor said that if Vado did not make a contract with the company and paid the debt himself it would take 61 years and add up to a total of $130,000. The math was somewhat suspect and the counselor discussed no up-front fees. The counselor was willing to set-up the account immediately. No reference was made as to the creditworthiness of Vado. The counselor stated there was no need for Vado to give the CCCS firm the credit card account numbers. There were five listings in the phone book for this same firm under debt consolidation, debt counseling, debt management, debt relief, and debt settlement. Although the counselor stated the company's location as being in New England this author suspected it was an overseas location.

The next call was to a number that was disconnected yet cycled over to a second number. When the party answered I could hear children's voices in the background. The suspicion was that it was a private residence. The counselor stated the firm would need Vado's credit report, also that the principle could be reduced and that the interest could be relieved completely. Note the word *could*, and not the word *would* was used. The cost of the service was $350 cash or check. The telephone listing stated that the debt would be erased. The six numbers in the Tucson phone book led to only two firms. The seventh call made was to a listing for Debtors Anonymous and the number was constantly busy.

Upon a search for debt relief counseling that was not a debt collection entity, two venues were discovered. A pastor stated his church, on two occasions, taught the Dave Ramsey Financial Peace University Program. However, the church offered the congregation no debt or debtor's group counseling. Then, realizing gamblers run-up huge credit card debt a sponsor for Gambler's Anonymous (GA) was called.

> GA offers a pressure relief group after 60 days of being gambling free. "The gambler in recovery must fill-out some forms, get a sponsor, and meet with trained debt counselors," to begin the path to lessening credit card debt. GA is a 12-Step program modeled after AA. The difference being the gambler must fill-out a detailed form; AA has no such requirement, and the gambler must stay in the groups. The gambler will get support from the group in addition to the counseling. The sponsor stated "the failure rate is very high."

And lastly, an attorney's office was called. The firm was advertised to be a bankruptcy firm. However, in smaller print at the bottom of the Yellow Page advertisement the statement was made that the firm was a debt counseling service. The staff member offered no advice, nor any other information over the phone. The advertisement stated that there was no charge for the first meeting.

The internet is replete with information about CCCS scams. Almost all listed credit score repair scams are the number one culprit as writer Mark Riddix pens in an article for financialedge.com.

> " ... companies often charge up-front fees costing you hundreds of dollars and promise to clean your credit up overnight ... or get a creditor to forgive your debt." The Federal Trade Commission (FTC) warns that "many of the claims those companies make; that they can remove judgments (and) liens," are a scam. Also, "file segregation ... to obtain new taxpayer identification or new employer identification numbers from the IRS

under false pretenses" is offered. This is a felony. (infoplease.com).

The card holder will pay fees for all this assistance. Another scam is for the CCCS to offer to send the debtor a check for double the consolidated monthly payment to pay the creditor for two months. The check comes with one stipulation and that is the client must send a separate check for half that amount, to begin an escrow account. The original check will come back as having non-sufficient funds and the debtor will be out the money sent to the escrow account. This is typical of scams of Nigerian origin.

In the investigation into counseling, I discovered that there is no credit counseling for debtors that is not really debt collection, or an outright confidence game. The counseling offered for debtors in 12-Step programs is pedestrian at best and may lead to sponsors offering very bad advice.

The Responsibility of Finance

"Debt is the worst poverty."
Thomas Fuller

This chapter is not about the parties responsible for paying credit card debt once incurred. It is about the parties responsible for plastic credit card binging that leads to a personal financial bubble burst. Credit card debt could lead to a national economic crisis likened to the 2008 banking debacle. The 2008 crash was caused by sub-prime mortgages; the next crisis could be caused by sub-prime lending and little plastic cards.

> The McKinsey Global Institute in a report released in 2010, "Blamed the middle-(income) consumers … (it seems) the international banking community and Wall Street have been looking for a way to deflect the blame of the global economic crisis for quite some time now … (it is a) financial system that seems unwilling to take responsibility for the current conditions."

As explained by Suze Orman, studies have shown that consumers will spend more when using a credit card. But a look at how a credit card bubble can be blown up, deals with some simple truths. Not including the card holders that can live on current income this thesis has taken the investigation to some new realities. Looking at the case study of Vado Allacani, the reader can see that at $46,000 a year Vado did not need a house with a $1,700 a month mortgage, or a BMW with a $425 per month payment, or $36,000 worth of over-the-limit credit card debt. Vado has made many financial mistakes. Vado could be living in an apartment, have bought a reasonably priced car, and charged only what could be paid-off each month.

But, in looking at another case study of someone forced to use a credit card the situation can be better understood. The average four year college graduate will have accumulated $20,000 in student loan and credit card debt, according to 2010 census data. Many students return home to live as there is no other choice. There is, however, a real problem for the graduate that has a job out-of-town and must move to begin a work life. The graduate will need an apartment with a deposit and first month's rent, phone and utility deposits, furniture, and perhaps a car. Even if public transportation is used the cost per month could be over $100. If a car is purchased, the payments will be due monthly, as will be the insurance costs. The list also includes necessities and perhaps a large output of funds for clothing. By the time the graduate is walking through the door on the first day of work the former student now has $30,000 in consumer debt. Most likely the graduate will have a modest, entry level salary.

Another case study is a high school classmate of the college graduate that did not go on to further schooling. The high school student went on to a job as a fork-lift driver in a warehouse. It is a union job and the fork-lift driver has vacation time, sick time, and medical insurance that goes with the union contract; great benefits all. So to, the fork-lift driver has an entry level job with a very moderate starting wage. The salary is so low the fork-lift driver can get but one credit card with a $3,000 maximum. The driver lives in an apartment and owns a used car. As it turns out, at twenty-two, the fork-lift driver is much further ahead, financially, than the college graduate. Without overburdening debt to pay-down the fork-lift driver would be far ahead of the college graduate by years, perhaps decades.

The case studies relate to personal responsibility and not the financial system. The system encompasses the banks, finance companies, and associations that offer and issue credit cards at rates beyond what would be considered usury. 29.99% interest or higher is appalling and is at the very crux of the consumer credit problem. However, since the public, in great numbers, applies for the cards and agrees to the terms such as rates set by *business strategies* and *for any reason*; is not the applicant responsible? How much can regulations protect the consumer? The economy of the US is based on supply and demand, and, what the market will bear. It appears the general public, the middle-income consumer, is willing to bear high APRs.

Regulating agencies are bureaucracies and do not function to the benefit of the consumer as the laws the agencies enforce are historically weak and full of loop-holes. The Consumer Financial Protection Bureau (CFPB) created during the first term of President Obama by now Senator Elizabeth Warren, was developed explicitly to protect the consumer. The bureau has done nothing to curb America's usury problem. The CFPB is now embroiled in a fight between the courts and Obama's appointment of the CFPB director during, or perhaps not during, a recess of Congress. It appears, in a Wall Street Journal article, that the priority of the CFPB is to keep Richard Cordray in the directorship position. And, until the matter is settled, the regulations developed under Cordray's directorship may be null and void. The question is; is the government responsible for overwhelming consumer debt? Has the government been lax or even incompetent in the matter of credit card rates being astronomical? Is it really up to the CFPB and like entities to protect the consumer from a 29.99% interest rate? The CFPB makes it appear that it is the enemy of debt as the documentary *In Debt We Trust* calls it. Or, as expressed in *The Card Game* that the "underlying problem (is) consumer confusion or (an uneducated public." The CFPB was a cause celebre for years during the development of the bureau, but has turned out to be a disappointment.

If the consumer or the student or the government is not responsible, perhaps it's the banks? It is the banking industry that throws millions at politicians and fills the representatives' coffers at the state and federal level. The reward for doing so is not favorable regulation but no regulation. In 1999, President Clinton signed into law a bill that legislated against regulating derivatives. It was a law against doing something about a future financial problem that caused the 2008 banking crisis as is discussed in *The Warning*, a documentary by Michael Kirk. Banks, as with any other businesses, will attempt to make the highest return on investment with the least expenditure. And it is working. The publically held bank's executives are responsible to the shareholders and corporate bond investors. The greater the bottom-line, the higher the firm's value, the higher will be equities. Also, the banks bond ratings will improve to garner more investment.

Unlike 2008 the banks are now flush with cash. The reason for this is the Federal Reserve has set very low, near zero, interest rates. Because of that the banks are not lending. Why should banks loan money at .03% when the credit card borrowing is at 29.99%, as is pointed out in the documentary *Inside the Meltdown*.

Perhaps the economy as a whole is at fault. As discussed in *The Crash Course* and *Capitalism Hits the Fan*, the wages of middle-income Americans have been flat since the mid-1970s. To maintain a middle-class lifestyle borrowing is the short-term answer. Consumers agreeing to 29.99% interest are not thinking of the long-term ramifications.

> The use of plastic as stated in *In Debt We Trust* means that "people are spending fake money." From *The Card Game* the viewer hears that "eventually (the consumer will) crash and burn if (they) keep borrowing." And, in *Mind Over Money* the warning is when the "individual bubble bursts (it will be) just like the financial crisis (of 2008)."

It is human nature to want to point a finger and say the simple solution is to blame one person, or one establishment, or one politician when it comes to consumer debt. Is it not one, but all, who are responsible?

Or, is it a lack of understanding on the part of the card holder? Or, is it an attitude of not caring on the part of the consumer?

"It's the economy, stupid."
James Carville

It is ingrained in our culture that massive debt is now acceptable. No longer is it shocking to hear a tale much like that of the case study Vado Allacani. Did you wince when seeing the $36,000 of credit card debt of Vado? That sort of debt, that high amount of debt, now, appears to be the new normal. Is it the new norm for a middle-income wage earner to have tens of thousands of dollars in revolving credit card debt? Is it the new norm to want more and more *stuff* simply to have more and more *stuff*? Raging consumer spending has evolved to be normal over the past thirty years. And, as the decades of 29.99% interest consumer debt builds, the country is becoming poorer and poorer for it. "The culture of poverty is the culture of consumer debt," *The Card Game*.

Sorry! The lifestyle you ordered is currently out of stock

The Resolution of Arrears

"Every Thing I Own."

Boy George, (Song title)

A warning; when a credit card holder is a co-signer, the co-signer is as responsible for the debts of that credit card as the original signer. Parents who co-sign children's credit card applications do two things. One, they are assuring the card will be issued to the child unless the parents' credit denies the card. The second; is the responsibility the parents take on to assure payment. Thus, the parents are assuring payment after the spending spree at the mall adjacent to the college or for those dorm pizza parties. The child can be an authorized user and not be responsible for the monthly payments. Tanisha Warner in her Credit Care column writes,

> " ... an authorized user ... is not financially responsible for the amount due; as a joint owner (the card holder) is responsible." A co-signer is the same as a joint owner. The joint owners' payment performance will affect their credit scores. An authorized user will not incur any credit score impact; either negative or positive.

When a parent co-signs a credit card account they will most likely foot the bill. If the student is issued a card, and has no income, the parents will ultimately foot the bill anyway. So, the parents must weigh the advantages and disadvantages of co-signing, or having the student on the card as an authorized user. Or, let the student strike out into the world with a credit card or two in hand. As is pointed out in *In Debt We Trust* the student may have an "intention to pay, but no way to do so." In a Wall Street Journal item by Kelly Greene, the author writes, about a parent who says, "You work your whole life and never pay a bill late … you don't ever think your kid isn't going to pay." The student, her daughter, had accumulated $55,000 in credit card debt and walked away leaving her mother, the co-signer, with the mess to clean up. Co-signing a child's credit card no matter whether a teenager or thirty-five year old is a sign of two things. One, if the child has no way to pay the monthly bill in the first place the co-signer will be stuck with the bills. Therefore, the question must be asked, why co-sign in the first place? Having anyone on a credit card as a joint owner or co-signer, is the same thing. It bears the same responsibility. Second, having a person on a card as an authorized user is still having the card owner bear the responsibility for payment. But, the advantage to the second option of authorized user is that the over-spending student can be removed from the account without canceling the card.

If trepidation is the prime emotion when addressing a credit card issue for any applicant it should be viewed as a red-flag. There are two methods to avoid the 29.99% interest that may be in the card holder's future. One, don't get a card in the first place. That is a simple solution and rather sophomoric. The reality is that a credit card, debit card, or a pre-paid card is necessary in today's society. More will follow about debit and pre-paid cards. A student cannot order less expensive used books online without a plastic card. A sales executive cannot book a flight or rent a car without a credit card. It has not happened yet, but in the future there will come a time when businesses will be cash and check free. Business' windows will display a sign that says something like 'plastic only'. Even today, writing checks has become archaic.

The second method left for prevention of credit card debt is to budget to spend no more on the card than can be paid for at the end of the billing cycle. A way to do this is to use an American Express card with the month-in-full payment stipulation. If the student cannot make the payment the first month the card will be canceled. The account will have added charges but the card cannot be used. The card holder is cut off from credit. This is not so with Discover, Visa, or MasterCard. These card's issuers are just waiting for the card holder's spending to get out of hand on that shopping spree or Spring-break trip. The idea may come to mind to get a card and not charge anything on it unless it is an emergency. Just activating a card will lower a FICO score. Again, Tanisha Warner,

> "Opening the new credit card account may cause a slight dip in your credit score. That's because FICO credit scores and other scoring models take into account how many times you've applied for credit in the recent past and how many times you've been

approved. The scoring models see applications for more credit as making you potentially risky."

Oddly enough getting a credit card and not using it may lower your FICO score, but if the card holder, even though not using the card, gets an increase in a card's limit it may improve the credit scores. This is because the debt-to-limit ratio is lower. But having a card for emergencies can be hazardous. It is amazing how a new fishing rod or a new perm, cut, and color can become an emergency.

If the credit card holder cannot pay the card off in one month the easy answer would be to stop charging and pay the card off as quickly as possible. The interest that will be accrued will be lower than the 29.99% used as punishment for the card being over-the-limit or a payment being late. Again, to stop charging is the resolution. But at all costs the card holder should stay below the limit. The fishing rod may turn in to a trip to Key West and the new hair-style may turn in to a fashion make-over on Fifth Avenue. The ability to pay will be the stressor at the end of the month. Affluence certainly helps. If the card holder has hundreds of thousands of dollars in the bank and in investments, the monthly rate on that card holders account will be lower. If the card holder is the thesis case study, Vado Allacani, the rate will be 29.99% or higher. Even if the affluent shopper is paying 10.99% on a contract that states 13.99% will be charged for cash withdraws, the first trip to the ATM will jump all charges on the bill to 13.99%; it is in the small print. What sets the rates are essentially two things, assessed ability to pay, and history of payments. The fact is the poor pay more.

> "The affluent pay less – those operating close to the margin are paying the most." (*The Card Game*) The documentary *MaxedOut* points to a mother and her disabled son given a liar-loan mortgage and they were in foreclosure. The bank administering the foreclosure sent them a loan application, pre-approved, for $5,000 with monthly payments at $129.

There was no mention of the length of the term of the loan. She wanted the loan and when asked why she would take the loan knowing she was unable to pay it back she replied, "But I'd have some money in my pocket."

Secured credit cards are, on the surface, an ideal method to have the convenience of a credit card yet not get into trouble with penalties. Or, at least, that is the thought of the card bearer upon first look. But, that is not so for a card holder that cannot pay-off the full amount each month. An investopedia.com explanation of a secured credit card is as follows;

> "Secured credit cards are known as pay-as-you-go cards. Upon opening the account, the card holder deposits a few hundred to a couple of thousand dollars. This determines the card holder's credit line. The limit is often based on a percent of the deposit which is usually 50-100% of what

you put into the account. The cards have an annual fee and higher annual interest rates. Most often, these cards are used to reestablish credit."

Why pay interest or annual fees against the money that the card holder has in the bank in the first place? If the card holder does not pay-off the full amount each month the card holder is charged interest on their own funds. Why not buy a pre-paid card and not take the chance of late and over-the-limit fees?

"Sunlight is the best disinfectant."

Louis Brandeis

Admitting the problem is best expressed in the Debtor's Anonymous Step One of the 12-Steps. "We admitted we were powerless over debt – that our lives had become unmanageable." There is a fifteen question list on the DA Website. Some of them relate to more than just the overwhelming debt but relate to the family and health of the debtor.

"Are your debts making your home life unhappy? Do your debts cause you to think less of yourself? Does the pressure of your debts make you careless of the welfare of your family? Does the pressure of your debts cause you to have difficulty sleeping? Has the pressure of your debts ever caused you to consider getting drunk? Do you justify your debts by telling yourself that you are superior to the other people, and when you get your break you'll be out of debt overnight?"

As with Gamblers Anonymous (GA) discussed earlier DA has pressure relief groups. To belong to the group the debtor must not have incurred unsecured debt for ninety days. In the pressure program the debtor's financial situation is reviewed and spending plans and action plans are formulated. With the exception of psychiatric or psychological care the only counseling I could find was Gamblers and Debtors Anonymous. After attending a DA meeting I found the examples of the case study Vado and The Family with $16,000 in credit card debt to be very close to the truth. The members took turns reading the twelve steps, again, the first step being "We admitted we were powerless over debt – that our lives had become unmanageable."

At first read, the DA member may be inclined to think of being a powerless victim. Over a period of DA meetings with the powerless mantra repeated the idea of being a victim of weakness is ingrained. Admitting powerlessness is a starting point of gaining power to take action against the debt. Day by day the debtor repeats powerlessness and therein is the misunderstanding, and the debtor remains in an unmanageable life spiral of debt. Nothing is accomplished by attending meetings and sharing the same sad tale over and over. This is not fault finding but reality. As a former New Hampshire State Prison drug and alcohol counselor I had experiences with the pitfalls of the 12-Steps. Considering powerlessness as a part of an incurable disease is an excuse to continue the self-defeating behavior. The repetition of creating more debt upon more debt and buying more and more *stuff* is an aberration of behavior. Admitting the problem is the beginning of getting out of debt but it can also be just admitting the problem without action.

There are methods for getting out from under credit card debt but the solutions are not miracles and are not a way to resolve the problem over night. In looking into methods of acquiring funds to pay-off the cards and consolidate the cost into one payment I found some terrible solutions. The solutions would have the card holder fall into a pit deeper than the original credit card debt. In fact, debt resolution firms create much more debt than the cards created, even with late and over-the-limit fees.

"At the time all acts of desperation seem logical."
Leonard Nimoy as Spock, Star Trek

Borrowing more money at interest to pay-off the credit cards is unsound. Borrowing money at interest makes no sense. If, however, the debtor can get a line-of-credit with a low APR it may be the best venue to pay-off the cards. The interest rate of the line-of-credit would have to be very low to have this tactic be effective. There are other avenues that can be used to borrow the large sums needed by a debtor in too deep. But, for the most part, the methods seem disastrous.

Home equity loans are for those fortunate enough to have value above the mortgage owed on a home. Borrowing against equity may be the less expensive way to pay down debt but it means the borrower will end up paying more for the home. Plus, in the economy of 2013, many homes are underwater and have no equity.

Pay-day loans and car title loans can be lumped into the scam category. Researching the title loan business I discovered an outrageously usurious scheme. The scam and scheme is this. When I called I was told by the loan officer that a car worth $9,000 with a free title could qualify for a loan of $25,000 when the title was surrendered. Further, the loan officer went on to say that the interest would be 10%. When asked if the 10% was the APR the reply was;

> "No, 10% per month." "That is $2,500 per month," was my reply. "That's right." I was so taken aback

by this that the amount of principle owed per month was not even discussed. Principle at this stage of debt would be a moot point. If the borrower missed one payment the car title loan company took possession of the car and the borrower owed $25,000 with interest payments amounting to $30,000 per year. "When people face hard problems they make mistakes." (*Mind Over Money*)

The case studies of Vado Allacani and The Family do not have these options as there is no home equity and their credit scores are too low for a line-of-credit loan. Also, their cars have no free title. Pay-day loan firms exist in 35 states and DC. The only difference between a pay-day loan and a title loan is the surrender of the title. Over a title loan pay-off period of six years, if the principle was paid at $348 plus the 10% owed per month, the total interest cost would be in the neighborhood of 600% which is the same for pay-day loans. "If you are in a jam you do what you have to do," says a woman at a pay-day loan office going in to borrow money to pay on a credit card. (*The Card Game*)

The idea of paying-off credit cards one at a time is advice found in get out of debt books. Whether to pay-off the lowest amount due card first or the highest amount due first is up to the card holder. Or, whether to pay-off the card with the highest interest first is also up to the debtor. The card holder can pay the over-the-limit card first as well. I offer no solutions. It is up to the consumer to resolve the debt.

Now to bankruptcy and the figures listed in bankruptcyaction.com. If the debtor has no funds or no income a bankruptcy lawyer may be out of the question. Non-business bankruptcies in the US are rampant. According to the census of 2010 data:

> "... bankruptcies have risen from 597,965 in 2006 to 5,536,799 in 2010;" an increase of 257%. For the case studies of Vado and The Family; bankruptcy may be the only recourse.

Bankruptcy is a way to restructure debt. Since the George W. Bush administration, bankruptcy is no longer just an easy way to absolve the debtor of all responsibility to pay. Sometimes debt is incurred as a result of circumstances beyond the control of the debtor. Fewer than 9% have suffered a job loss, medical event or divorce."

Thus, 91% are in bankruptcy court because of out-of-control spending. Bankruptcy is a legal matter. I offer no advice as to whether to declare bankruptcy. It is up to the consumer to resolve the debt.

The court's doors swing both ways. The debtor may be able to walk away from the debt or may have it restructured more to the benefit of the card issuers. If court action is not an option for the card holder should the debtor just stop paying? Doing so will skyrocket the debt. Doing so will also garner myriads of collection strategies used against the debtor in the forms of letters demanding payment, threats of legal action, and phone calls at all times of the day and night. I could find no statistics as to borrowers being brought into legal proceedings or the debt eventually being written-off by the issuer. Stopping payment would be an act of desperation on the part of the debtor.

In the documentary *In Debt We Trust* there is a segment about a church that takes up collections to pay off the debt of its members. How the debtors are selected was not expressed. The idea that over-the-limit cards get paid down first would be difficult to resolve as a high percentage of credit card holders are over-the-limit.

Consumers are abandoning credit cards for debit cards. However, a debit card can be used to charge beyond the amount of funds in the account and thus an over-the-limit fee is charged much as a check over-draft. The exception is that the use of the debit card does pay for the debit against the account where the amount of the check will not be paid but returned. The account holder with the check over-draft is charged a fee but the check receiver is out the money and also charged a fee. Also, a debit account will have a limit on the amount of over-draft and eventually the card will be rejected. (The Card Game) Using debit cards are a protection against accumulating out of control debt.

Another plastic card that can be used to prevent credit card debt and debit card over-draft fees is the pre-paid credit card. These cards are not really credit cards. Pre-paid cards can be used only for the amount of the card. The card has the same features with embossed numbers and a magnetic strip. However, there is no name on the card. The cards can be seen in stores offering Visa, Discover, American Express, and MasterCard. Also, there will be cards offered for a host of businesses such as online vendors and local restaurants. Once the dollar limit of the card is reached the card becomes invalid. There is a cost for these cards and the rate is high, but not as high as a credit card. For a $25 card the charge is $3.95 which is a 16% one-time fee. This is a much better rate than a 16% revolving charge; and far better than a 29.99% usurious monthly charge. It is up to the consumer to decide the best card for commerce.

The Philosophy of Preservation

Vado Allacani and The Family are irrationally selfish. Their irrational selfishness is leading to their own destruction. Or, in reality, they have already created their own calamity. They are beyond the control of their own finances and the credit card issuer has taken over and is draining them of their money. The banks are reaching into their pockets and taking out every last cent. They will work until they are dead and leave debt behind them as a legacy of their struggle and depression and fear of having nothing yet wanting more.

Capital can be retained by the earning of money paid to the worker for their time and effort and saved. Capital can also be gained illegally, through theft or fraud. Capital can also be acquired by borrowing. It is borrowing that meets the demand and supply chain of the consumer. If enough consumers demand an item of exchange, either a product or a service, a supply will be generated to meet the need. The same function exists for credit. The more the consumer wants, the more credit will be offered. And, it is easy for the banks to supply the demand. They need produce nothing, only raise the limit on an existing card or issue new cards to those sending in the solicitations received in the mail. It is that easy. And, it is easy for the consumer to keep demanding the credit until the supply of personal credit is used up and the cards are over-the-limit. That is where the banks want the consumer to be and that is where the consumer irrationally goes. Yes, those overwhelmed with consumer debt are irrational. The book, so far, outlines debt, defines debt, gives extreme examples of credit card debt, and reveals statistics of a consumer culture derelict in improving their financial IQs. Not understanding the exponential factoring required to calculate compound interest upon compound interest is a lack of basic understanding of the threat to your personal finances. And, the compounding of interest should be learned in high school. To learn it in college is too late as the credit cards are already in the pockets of freshmen as of registration day.

Sharon Lechter, a resident of Tucson, Arizona, devotes time and great effort to helping consumers understand credit card debt. Arizona State Senator Kimberly Yee, R-Phoenix, has introduced legislation that requires an understanding of personal finance before a high school diploma will be awarded. Kudos to both ladies.

What has the debt ridden consumer done to get to the stage of overwhelming debt? They have created anxiety and brought fear into their psyches that will be with them 'til the end of their time. To buy and buy and buy thinking the purchases and *stuff* will make them happy, will, in the end, become a quick fix, ending in a psychological hollowness. Ayn Rand wrote,

> "Happiness is that state of consciousness which proceeds from the achievement of one's values. If a man values productive work, his happiness is the measure of his success in the service of his life. But if a man values destruction, like a sadist – or self-torture like a masochist – or life beyond the grave, like a mystic – or mindless 'kicks' like the driver of a hotrod car (or a buyer of a 100-inch flat screen TV on credit) – his alleged happiness is the measure of his success in the service of his own destruction … a moment's relief from … chronic terror." Rand goes on to say, "Neither life nor

happiness can be achieved by the pursuit of irrational whims. Just as man is free to attempt to survive by any random means … he is free to seek happiness in any irrational fraud, any whim, any delusion, any mindless escape from reality … but not free … to escape the consequences."

Consumers immersed in credit card debt fall into that pit by not being selfish but by being irrationally selfish. Selfishness is the one quality that will benefit US citizenry, especially debtors, more than any other attribute. Selfishness is good. As Rand writes, Selfishness is "concern with one's own interests."

Noah Webster's dictionaries define selfish as "motivated by personal desires while disregarding the feelings of others, concerned excessively or exclusively with oneself: seeking or concentrating on one's own advantage, pleasure, or well-being without regard for others …"

Why would you care about someone else's feelings when it comes to your money? As discussed earlier the feeling of helplessness and the assumed powerlessness of being in debt to great to be able to pay it down, much less pay it off, is not being in the service of oneself. Do you think the credit card issuers care how you feel? Have you ever felt that the employee servicing your account was upset because you were late with a payment? No! What being late with the payment means is that the next payment will be for more interest and less principle! Then the card issuers have you exactly where they want you in relation to the account. The credit card issuers are selfish. They concentrate upon their own advantage. This is capitalism and it is the motive behind the quest for profits.

Let's take a short detour into socialism. It is a socialist idea to think that some outside entity is going to come along and pay your debts. Socialism, according to Webster, is collective or government control. Socialism is the enemy of capitalism. In a socialistic society the consumer has very little access to credit. What would be the government's motivation? It makes no sense to reap money from the very people it is paying and have the interest owed the government. The consumer in a collective society has everything they need provided for them and credit would only expand their materialism to getting what they want. The government cares not what someone wants only what they need. The government will not consider a 100-inch flat screen TV a need. You may even have to do with a black and white with vacuum tubes. In socialism there is no motivation for the collective to make a profit. No government has ever done so. So, only in a capitalist society can a middle-income, working class, consumer have access to almost unlimited credit. What brought about a US capitalist system was our forefathers changing of the governments function from the "role of ruler to the role of servant," writes Ayn Rand in her book *The Virtue of Selfishness*. Thus, the consumer waiting for the government to come along and save them from sixteen to thirty-six thousand dollars worth of credit card debt are wishing to be ruled by a political class who are not inclined to keep the government a servant of the people.

Socialism is the redistribution of wealth and if the middle-income, working-class consumer thinks that the money will only be taken from the wealthy to provide for the poor perhaps they will take the time to give a thought to this. There are millions and millions more poor US citizens then there are wealthy citizens to support them. So, the encroachment of the socialists will begin at, perhaps, the million dollar annual income mark and when that does not provide enough for the poor, the incomes of those at five hundred thousand may be tapped, then two hundred thousand, then the government will dig deeper and go into the pockets of the fifty thousand per year wage earner. And, it will all be to support the low-income and no wage earning strata of the US population. Under socialism the rich get poorer and the middle-income wage earners get poorer, and the poor get poorer. Everyone else is worse off. But the government functionaries will live off taxation and get fatter and fatter from eating out of the public trough.

Government control of the banks to benefit the consumers with so much credit card debt means the government will force the banks to take action against their own best interests. That will not happen in a capitalist model of banking. Hoping the government will come along and force the banks to lower your interest rates to make your monthly payments lower is a pipe dream. It is wishful thinking. It is akin to the powerlessness expressed in the rooms of the Debtors Anonymous meetings.

Are you of the altruistic belief that all mankind is the keeper of their brothers and sisters? Altruism goes but one way. Taking from the haves to give to the have-nots. The have-nots are not altruistic – they only take. So, should the federal government force wage earners to support what will become the largest culture in America – the non-working population. Again, pens Ayn Rand,

> "The moral cannibalism of all hedonist and altruist doctrines lies in the premise that the happiness of one man necessitates the injury of

another." And, further she writes, "The meaning of John Galt's statement in *Atlas Shrugged* that the alleged shortcut to knowledge, which is faith, is only a short cut to destroying the mind."

The idea that the government or Elizabeth Warren will provide an answer to your personal financial problems is compounding the powerlessness of feeling you have no solution. The fact is you may have no solution. Rand writes, "There is only one reality – the reality knowable to reason." In case you have not recognized it by now, this chapter is about retaining your wealth and the objectivism you will need to cope with your debt and understand how you can get you out of it.

How is it that the bank charges you 29% or 39% or 49% interest? It is because they can, and because you are willing to take on such a debt load, and, because the credit demand exists and the money supply supports it.

Altruism is not charity. Altruism is not giving an extra tip to a college student waitress. Altruism is not having the high school kid mow your lawn for ten dollars when you can do it yourself. That is not charity either. It is commerce. Altruism is not commerce. Buy a 100-inch flat screen TV on a lay-away plan over a course of a couple of pay-days is commerce for both the buyer and the seller. Buying the TV on a credit card of which you cannot afford the monthly minimum payments is commerce for the seller, but it is servitude for the buyer. The 'man' I wrote about earlier, well, you are workin' for him. And it is the CEO of the banks from which your credit cards come. Who, you know; get those $9 million bonuses. The amount really looks like this - $9,000,000.

If you owe more annually than you earn annually – you are poor. You just don't know it yet because poverty has not caught up with you; yet. A big house, SUVs, a big boat, and those thousands of dollars in country club dues mean, "you are up to your eyeballs in debt." But instead of the altruistic wealthy CEO bailing you out of debt and giving you a living; it is the opposite. You, the new poor, and that is what you are, are supporting 'the man'. The debt train has just left the station in the opposite direction than you expected it to go. You are creating your own unhappiness at your own expense and the CEOs are living in the Hamptons and flying on private jets. That is what capitalism is. It is a system of profit and loss. It makes people wealthy or it gives others the opportunity to go broke and perhaps start over again. There are no guarantees for the capitalists. The 99% squabble about the 1%. You do not have to become part of the 1% to gain happiness in service to yourself. Just join the top 49% that are wealthy enough to pay taxes.

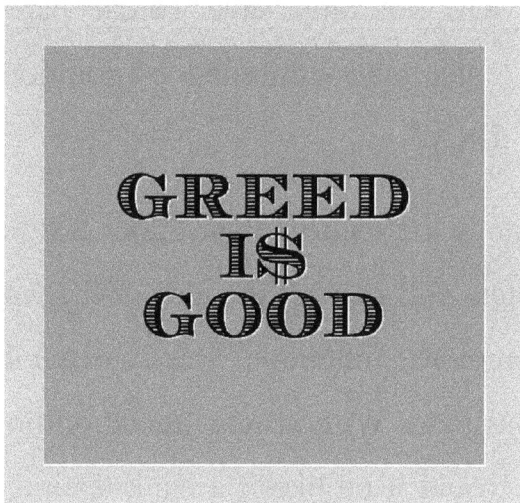

The Culture of Debt

Michael Douglas as the character Gordon Gekko in the movie *Wall Street* never said greed is good. What he said was,

"Greed, for the lack of a better word, is good. Greed works. Greed clarifies, cuts through, and captures the essence of the evolutionary spirit. Greed, in all of its forms, greed for life, for money, for love, knowledge, has marked the upward surge of mankind, and greed, you mark my words, will not only save Teldar Paper, but that other malfunctioning corporation called the USA."

Exchange the name Teldar Paper for the American banking system and you get the idea of the way money in capitalist commerce functions. Money is the life-blood of American business. Without capitalization no firm could exist. What would it be like if a bank leveraged itself by investing forty dollars to each one dollar in deposits? Well, that is exactly what the commercial and investment banks did. The Federal Reserve channeled billions through JPMorgan Chase into Bear Stearns to save it from default. Bank of America bought Merrill Lynch for the same reason. Lehman Brothers could not be saved and disappeared into the shadows of bankruptcy.

Why am I telling you this? Why should a credit card holder know this? It is because no matter how much the credit card debtor hopes for a windfall it will not be there. There is no Federal Reserve, no Credit Card Reserve to bail you out. The Federal Reserve is there to serve as a reserve currency provider for the US banking system. It has been doing so since 1913.

During our still on-going Great Recession the administration attempted to enact programs to relieve mortgage holders of their payments and lower the rates of interest. This was to be done by two venues. One, reduce the interest of the loan. And two, reduce the appraised value of the home and reset the loan to fit it. The banks would hear none of it. The mortgagees signed the documents and they are required to pay the loan in full. Thus, comes the thought process on the part of those sub-prime mortgagees that 'at least the bank is getting something, isn't that better than the banks getting nothing'. So, why didn't the banks make the deals? Because, to do so the banks would lose money. It is that simple. If the banks would have come to the conclusion that they would make money by lowering the interest or by resetting the principle they would have done so.

The mortgage crisis was a macro-case of the credit card state of affairs. The banks will not reset principles, nor will they lower interest rates, as doing so will lessen their income; their return on investment and their bottom line. So, have you come to the conclusion that the banks are greedy; "Greed, for the lack of a better word, is good … greed is the essence of the evolutionary spirit." Simply stated the banker's do not care if Vado Allacani has $122 to live on month to month; they want their money. And, legally they are entitled to it.

We are not a collectivist society. We do not have a socialist government. In the article "Collectivized Ethics" Ayn Rand writes,

> "What will be done about the poor … the altruist collectivist premise, implicit in that question, is that men are "their brothers keepers" and that the misfortune of some mortgage on others … once when Barbara Brandon

was asked by a student: "What will happen to the poor in a objectivist society" she answered: "If you want to help them you will not be stopped."

Therefore, as Brandon phrases it, charity will help the poor and disadvantaged, not altruism and a collective economy of socialism. Socialism is nothing more than self-imposed communism. Socialist governments as with Greece and Great Britain under the Labour Party are elected collectivism. And, it is just this collectivism that the 99% and the credit card debtors hope for. 'If someone will just come along and pay the bills' is another mantra.

Having faith in a miracle of debt relief is living in a world devoid of reality. How can the ideas of Ayn Rand be applied to reality, to reason, to rational thinking, and to the philosophy of Objectivism, or, as it can be restated – to objectivist thinking? Objectivist thinking is to understand that there are no contradictions. Or, as Rand expresses it "The art of non-contradictory identification." Any contradiction is,

"An idea not derived from reality, not validated by a process of reason, not subject to rational examination or judgment – and worse: an idea that clashes with the rest of one's concepts and understanding of reality. The conscious is sabotaged."

Having faith in the resolution of your debt by an irrational, unreasonable, contradictory outside element is greed of the psyche. It is not the "Greed, for the lack of a better word, is good," as says Gordon Gekko. It is unreasonable to think you can get out of debt by not being responsible for the debt. It is unreasonable to believe some outside force will alleviate the burden of your debt.

"What we've got here, is a failure to communicate."
Strother Martin as the Captain, Cool Hand Luke

When the credit card bill arrives there is a payment due amount and a due date specified on the notice. The issuer expects you to pay the monthly charge on the interest and principle and, perhaps, the over-the-limit fees and late charges. If you do not pay by the date the funds are due, you and the bank have a failure to communicate. You are sending an irrational message that you do not intend to pay. If the reason for the lack of payment is no funds available, or you just choose not to pay, you are communicating an irrational message. But, the message from you is clear to the credit card issuer; they are not getting any money. Thus, you have communicated unreasonably, irrationally, and thus, you failed to communicate a message of service to yourself. You have broken the contract you signed to get the credit. Now that you have the money you are, in your mind, voiding the contract. But, alas, you are fulfilling the contract that states any non- or late-payment will incur additional fees. You are owing more and more, as you pay less and less; very irrational and unreasonable.

It is beyond reason to think the bank will loan you tens of thousands of dollars and not expect you to pay it back. It is rational on their part to enter into a contract with the bearer of the card. It is irrational on the part of the bearer to believe that not paying is appropriate. Not to pay the monthly bill is not an option to the card bearer's benefit. It will only compound the problem. Isn't it something the way the word compounding keeps coming up in discussions about credit cards? You have the obligation to pay and the bank is obliged to add fees if you do not.

The irrational idea that the bank should not have advanced you the money as you are too great a credit risk is not an objective outlook. How did the bank come to understand that you were an acceptable risk? Were you willing to accept a higher rate of interest because you had a low FICO score? Obviously, you and the bank came to terms on the deal and the contract was agreed upon by both parties. If it appears I am stating the obvious to you; I am. If you understand the idea of rational, reasonable, and objective thinking toward consumer debt at this stage I have done well.

What is your motivation? What is your attitude? Those Adam Roarke questions came up earlier. Let's look at them as we look at greed. "Greed, for the lack of a better word (is not always) good." Face it, it was greed that got you sentenced to a life-term of debt. It was a 100-inch flat screen TV, it was a rack of designer fashions, or it was a cup of coffee and a piece of pie. Wanting something and using credit to buy it is acceptable and rational if the bill is paid in-full within the billing period. Wanting something and using a credit card to buy it, on sale, and then paying 29.99% interest on a delinquent account is not rational.

Credit cards are only rational if you pay no interest on the accounts. The credit card issuer's term for non-interest paying account holders is a *dead-beat.* Pay the bill on time and be a dead-beat. The banks will move on and squeeze 30% out of someone else. "Well, I couldn't afford that 100-inch flat screen TV when I wanted it," you say. Then don't buy it. Put it on lay-away. Do without. Because, in the long run, no, in a very short run you will do with less and less and the banks will have more and more of your money. I am not writing about a personal solution to your debt. I am writing about objective, rational, reasonable thinking. Frankly, I do not care if you owe everything you earn to 'the man'. You have to care.

Another irrational idea of credit card use is the notion that you can use credit cards to pay those monthly bills, or the car payment, or the rent. You will end up paying 29.99% more. All interest payments mean you are spending your earned income for nothing. Interest is the wind beneath the wings of the banks and it is your funds they are flying away with. It's time to get selfish. It's time to get greedy. It's time to be of service to yourself.

The Psyche of Selfishness

"Caution is the confidential agent of selfishness."
Woodrow Wilson

The cycle of debtors not being in service to themselves
continues card debt, and it is on the rise. In The Wall

Street Journal article, Households Return to Borrowing Ways by Neil Shah, is quoted,

> "Americans late last year took on more debt for the first time since the throes of the recession, a sign consumers are feeling more comfortable borrowing after years of cutting debt to fix their finances. Household debt, which includes mortgages, credit cards, and loans and student loans, rose 0.3% to $11.34 trillion in the fourth quarter – the first fundamental increase since the third quarter 2008."

From the third to the fourth quarter of 2012 the article shows graphs of home-equity loans falling 1.7%, credit cards rising 0.7%, auto loans rising 2.0%, and student loans rising 1.0%. It is obvious why home equity loans are down. It is because so many homes are underwater.

Four days preceding the Shah article was The Wall Street Journal article of 27 February 2013 by Whelan and Dougherty titled Builders Fuel Home Sale Rise. Two paragraphs of that article tell a chilling story of what could be the beginning of the US repeating the recent Great Recession's mortgage crisis. It reads,

> "In the past two years, more home builders have offered to pay closing costs and arrange home loans through in-house mortgage operations. They have hosted free credit-counseling sessions for buyers with bad credit, and made heavy use of government-backed mortgage programs that allow buyers to get a home with little or no down payment. The result is that for many buyers, it has become far easier to buy a new home than an existing one. It's as if people were going to the car dealership and realizing that there aren't any used junkers left, so they're buying shiny new SUVs, said Ivy

Zelman, an independent housing analyst" The article goes on to say, "buyers are biting off more than they can chew."

Does this sound familiar to you? Déjà vu – it's a step back in time. The Twilight Zone. One Step Beyond. It is the coming of the surreal world of lack of greed, that failure to be selfish, and the lack of being in service to oneself. It is a path leading to financial ruin once again; all because of the *I want it* syndrome. And, if the mortgagee or credit card bearer knows he or she does not have the ability to pay, it is a lawless loan. The contract is breached before the ink is dry on the paper. It is also a step Through The Looking Glass into the loss of self-respect.

> *"People who respect money tend to respect themselves more."*
> *Jonathan Hoenig, Business News Pundit*

Throwing out statistics to the reader may be effective for a paragraph or two, but that is it. From the documentary, *Prophets of Doom*, comes the idea that we think if we can measure something we can control it. We, us, the US citizenry, are staring into a pool of still water and we are falling in love with the reflection. We are Narcissus. We are falling in love with the five thousand square feet home. We are enamored by the swimming pool. We love the three car garage with a Lincoln, a BMW, and a Mercedes. We are so proud of the twenty-foot cabin cruiser we just financed and we sail on three weekends a year. But, of course, we have a huge picture of it in our screening room adjacent to the unoccupied servant's quarters.

While creating a personal financial problem we have, collectively, created a national financial problem. It has become more pronounced with underwater mortgages and student loan debt because that seems from whence the statistics flow. Just because the nation is in debt it does not mean we have to be in debt. The attitude of if the government doesn't care why should I; is irrational.

We should all care about bettering our greed and increasing our selfishness. We should all care about greed being good for us. We should all care about being very, very selfish. We should all have excessive acquisitiveness; be greedy. And, we should all have concern with our own interests; again, be selfish. If we are more selfish with our money there would be no interest to compound. If we kept our money to ourselves we would own our purchases and not have *stuff* for which to pay an additional 29.99%.

It is our lack of greed and lack of selfishness that has gotten us into this mess. If we were more greedy about our money we would owe less. If we were more selfish with our money we would only mortgage an affordable home and finance an affordable car; and not a cabin cruiser. Being financially fit is a result of greed and selfishness. Throwing away 29.99% above cost compounded monthly is *materialism* – a preoccupation with owning *stuff*.

Our national psyche, our national mind, one debtor at a time has got to turn to selfishness and greed or more and more of the US population will become immersed in debt so punishing the debtors will never see the light of day from the shadows of owing and owing.

I project it will take two generations to become accustomed to the words greed and selfish being positive. Who says greed is a deadly sin? It's nowhere in the bible. "Neither a borrower nor lender be" is not from the bible but from Hamlet. But it is great advice. "Money is the root of all evil" is not a quote from anything; it is a misbelief. From the Aramaic it is written,

> "... but the root of all these evils is the love of money, and there are some who have decried it and have erred from the faith and have brought themselves many miseries."

So, has debt brought many miseries? Greed and selfishness are not love. But greed and selfishness with your own money can bring about self-respect, and self-reliance. This is for many a new way of thinking, but how else can one not get into a debt crisis in the first place? The US economy is becoming our personal economy. That is what affects us, that is the important economy, not a far removed national budget. It is the kitchen table budget that has to be resolved. You can decide to live in misery or prevent it.

"Greed, for the lack of a better word, is good." Be greedy with your own money. Accumulate as much of your income as you can. Teach your children to keep money in the bank and not contribute it to some CEOs stock options bonus. Be selfish with your money. Don't give it away to persons who will do nothing but take and take. Altruism is a pox on the people. And, don't feel guilty about it. If you live within your means all will be better.

I have cautioned against accruing debt in a myriad of ways. I hope it sinks in for those that are able to prevent it, so you, your children, and your grandchildren can understand the benefits of greed and selfishness when it comes to personal finances, but what of those in debt way beyond the ability to pay it off. To those I offer no solution. You have to search for it yourself. There are options out there. Cut up the cards. Get a line-of-credit for a one time pay-off. Pay the highest bill first. Pay the lowest bill first. Pay the highest interest card first. Pay the lowest interest card first. Go to a commercial credit counseling service. Go to a non-profit credit counseling service. Sell your house and rent a less expensive apartment. Trade down on your overly expensive car. Get an extra part-time job. Ask your family for help. Go to Debtors Anonymous and work the steps. Declare bankruptcy. No debt guru or how-to author can lead you to the correct solution – you have to do it yourself! And, when you get out of debt; be greedy and selfish and don't do it again!

"I'm just selfish. I have to be for what I do."
Shia LaBeouf, as Jake Moore in, Wall
Street: Money Never Sleeps

"The problem of social organization is how to set up an arrangement under which greed will do the least harm, capitalism is that kind of system."
Milton Friedman, Nobel Prize recipient,
Economics

"The banking collapse was caused, more than anything, by bad government policy and the total failure of bad regulation, rather than greed."   Nigal Farage, *Leader of the UK Independence Party*

"It has always seemed strange to me ... those traits we detest, sharpness, greed, acquisitiveness, meanness, egotism and self-interest, are the traits of success ..." *John Steinbeck*

"Being stubborn has helped, being selfish is not a bad thing. Being selfish to me means that you have to look out for yourself and you don't have to sacrifice." *Herbie Mann, Musician*

"When Will They Learn" *Boy George (Song title)*

The banks, finance companies, associations, title loan firms, and pay-day loan corporations charge the consumer what the market will bear. Out of desperation the poor and unfortunate walk into loan stores and pawn shops. For the out-of-work and the ill perhaps there is no other choice. What I found out is that there are those in dire straits that have no choice but to take-out a 600%

interest loan. Or do they? Or, is it an avenue of least resistance? Or, are the loan companies simply preying on the people who are down on their luck? What appears to be quick and easy money only compounds the problem. Once the loan scammers get back 10% of the principle it is all return-on-investment for them. The signers and co-signers will pay and pay, perhaps for decades. The saying 'workin' for the man' is so true for those who fall in the pit of credit card debt. But, there are 91% of those who have spent themselves into ruination that declare bankruptcy. It is not the ill or the desperate that present the problem of consumer debt. It is the wage earner who is allowing 'the man', really 'the banks', to take their money for a lifetime. The problem has developed from their idea of materialism; the accumulation of *stuff*. It has evolved from the consumer wanting more and more. It has evolved from the consumer wanting the best, or the top-of-the-line. And, it has evolved into a problem of financial ruin and depression. This book is not about the 9% of bankruptcies caused by unfortunate events. I have written this about the preponderance of debtors who acquired tens of thousands of dollars of debt at an interest rate 29.99% or greater. They did it to themselves for home delivery pizza or a cup of coffee with a side of pie. The reason is more than keeping up with the Joneses. The reason is the feeling that plastic cards are not real money, until that is, the bills arrive. The reason is a quick fix and the thrill of shopping, spending, and acquiring goods of which the cost will double or triple as minimum payments are made. The reason is the idea of I deserve this. The reason for US consumer debt being over a trillion dollars is a sense of entitlement. Let's wrap this up with a quote from a column in the March 2013 issue of The Wall Street Journal Magazine, by Samantha Boardman, MD, a psychiatrist. She writes,

> "I think of discipline in the context of self-control. For a lot of us, it's hard to imagine anything besides 'I want it, and I want it now'. … Impulsive behavior is appealing: in the heat of the moment, you want that piece of cake or that pair of shoes, but you are not thinking about the consequences. Instant gratification can lead to

trouble … think … about your future self … we always have a choice."

According to Abraham Maslow self-actualizers have efficient perceptions of reality. "Self-actualizers are able to judge situations correctly and honestly. They are very sensitive to the fake and dishonest, and are free to see reality 'as it is'."

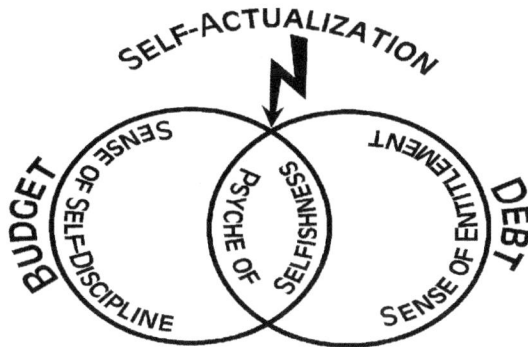

References

BankAmericard (2012) Retrieved from www.bankofamerica.com, on 5 June 2012

Bankruptcy (2011) US Bankruptcies 1980 – 2009, Retrieved fromhttp://bankruptcyaction.com, on 20 November 2011

Bergman, L., De Granados, O. (2009) *The Card Game*, Boston, MA, Frontline,WGBH Educational Foundation, DVD

Boardman, S. (March 2013) This month: Discipline, NYC, The Wall Street Journal

Chittum, R. (9 March 2012) 200 Years of Citi, Retrieved from http://www.cjr.org on 4 March 2013

Citi (2012) Retrieved from applyonline.citisimplicity.com, on 5 June 2012

Clark, M. (2010) *Mind Over Money*, Boston, MA, WGBH Educational Foundation, DVD

Consumer Debt Statistics (15 November 2011) Retrieved from http://www.money-zine.com, on 15 November 2011

Credit Card (2011) Retrieved from http://en.wikipedia.org

Credit Card Debt Statistics (2013) Retrieved from http://www.statisticsbrain.com, on 28 January 2013

Credit Card Pay-off Calculator (2013) Retrieved from http://www.moneychimp.com, on 28 January 2013

Credit Cards (2012) Retrieved from http://dmoz.org, on 5 June 2012

Credit Counseling (2011) Retrieved from http://www.bills.com, on 15 November 2011

Credit Sense (2013) How does credit card interest impact you? Retrieved from youtube.com, DVD

Debtors Anonymous (2013) 12-Steps and 15 Questions, Retrieved from http://www.debtorsanonymous.org, on 4 February 2013

Debt Consolidation Solutions (2011) Report: Consumers to blame for financial crisis. Retrieved from http://www.debtconsolidationsolutions.net Pages 1-2, on 17 November 2011

Federal Trade Commission (2011) The Top Five Consumer Debt Plans, Retrieved from http://www.infoplease.com, on 15 November 2011

Fowles, B. (2011) The Psychology of Spending Money, Retrieved from http://financialplan.about.com, on 19 November 2011

Gordon, S. (2010) *Freakonomics, The Movie*, LA, CA, Magnolia HomeEntertainment, DVD

History of the Discover Credit Card (2008) Did you know that Discover cards were the brainchild of Sears? Retrieved from http://creditcardforum.com on 4 March 2013

History of MasterCard Credit Cards, The (2008) Retrieved from http://creditcardforum.com, on 4 March 2013

History of Sears, Roebuck and Co (2013) Retrieved from http://www.fundinguniverse.com on 4 March 2013

Hull, J. (2013) Credit card debt and drug addiction: Are they related? Retrieved from http://www.hullfinancialplanning.com, on 29 January 2013

Killian, M. (16 September 2009) Are you in a money fog? The Psychology of Money and Credit Cards. Retrieved from http://www.cardratings.com, on 19 November 2011

Kirk, M. (2009) *Inside the Meltdown*, Boston, MA, WGBH Educational Foundation, DVD

Kirk, M. (2009) *The Warning*, Boston, MA, Frontline, WGBH Educational Foundation, DVD

Langione, J. (2009) *Canzio: A Sal Luca Gig*, Philadelphia, PA, Xlibris, Page 129

Lewis, M. (1991) *The Money Culture*, Leave Home Without It: The Absurdity of the American Express Card, NYC, W. W. Horton & Company, Pages 11-20

Loomis, J. (28 June 2006) MasterCard Changing Name, Retrieved from http://www.lohud.com, on 9 January 2013

MarksJarvis, G. (20 January 2013) Researchers find correlation between debt, depression. Tucson, AZ, Arizona Daily Star, Page D2

Martenson, C. (2008) *The Crash Course*, chrismartenson.com productions, DVD

MasterCard Incorporated (2010) Retrieved from http://www.sec.gov, on 9 January 2013

MasterCard Milestones (20 September 2011) Retrieved from http://www.mastercard.com, on 9 January 2013

Orman, S. (1997) *The 9 Steps to Financial Freedom*, NYC, Random House, Pages 29-30

Prophets of Doom (2011) A&E Television Networks LLC

Pulse (12 January 2005) Merger of Discover Financial Services and Pulse EFTAssociation, Retrieved from http://investorrelations.discoverfinancial.com, on 9 January 2013

Ramsey, D. (2013) What is Financial Peace University? Retrieved from http://www.daveramsey.com, on 1 February 13

Rand, A. (1961) *The Virtue of Selfishness*, NYC, Penguin Group

Riddix, M. (22 July 2010) 6 New Credit Scams to Watch-out For, Retrieved from http://financialedge.investopedia.com, on 15 November 2011

Roberts-Gray, G. (2 November 2009) Credit Card Addiction: How to spot the warning signs and break the habit. Retrieved from http://www.dailyfinance.com, on 29 January 2013

Roth, J. (22 August 2008) The Psychology of Credit Cards, Retrieved from http://www.getrichslowly.org, on 19 November 2011

Savage, T. (1999) *The Savage Truth on Money*, NYC, John Wiley & Sons, Pages 35-60

Savings Calculator (2013) Feeling really good about being kinda cheap, Retrieved from http://www.moneychimp.com, on 28 January 2013

Schecter, D. (2007) *In Debt We Trust*, NYC, GlobalVision Films, DVD

Schecter, D. (2010) *Plunder*, NYC, GlobalVision Films, DVD

Scurlock, J. (2007) *MaxedOut*, LA, CA, Magnolia Home Entertainment, DVD

Sears Brands LLC (12 August 2009) A Brief Chronology of Sears History, Retrieved from http://searsarchives.com, on 9 January 2013

Secure POS Vendor Alliance is Launched by Hypercom, Ingencio, and Verifone (2012) Retrieved from http://ecommerce-journal.com, on 5 June 2012

Shah, N. (1 March 2013) Households Return to Borrowing Ways, NYC, The Wall Street Journal, Page A2

Simon, J. (2013) Visa: a short history, Retrieved from http://www.creditcards.com on 4 March 2013

Sington, D. (2012) *The Flaw*, NYC, Studio Lambert, DVD

Stahl, L. (2009) Bank CEO Interview, NYC, 60 Minutes, CBS

Whelan, R., Dougherty, C. (27 February 2013) Builders Fuel Home Sale Rise, NYC, The Wall Street Journal, Front Page

Wolff, R.(2009) *Capitalism Hits the Fan*, Northhampton, MA, Media Education Foundation, DVD

Woolsey, B. (2013) The history of American Express, Retrieved from http://www.creditcards.com, on 4 March 2013

Zibel,A., Crittenden, M. (30 January 2013) Banks worry CFPB may be weakened, NYC, The Wall Street Journal, Page C3